BASIC ILLUSTRATED

Edible Wild Plants and Useful Herbs

Jim Meuninck

FALCON GUIDES

GUILFORD, CONNECTICUT
HELENA, MONTANA

AN IMPRINT OF GLOBE PEQUOT PRESS

To buy books in quantity for corporate use
or incentives, call **(800) 962-0973**
or e-mail **premiums@GlobePequot.com**.

FALCONGUIDES®

FalconGuides is an imprint of Globe Pequot Press.
Falcon, FalconGuides, and Outfit Your Mind are registered trademarks of Morris Book Publishing LLC.

Photos: Jim Meuninck, except beargrass, page 85, licensed by Shutterstock

Text design: Sheryl P. Kober
Layout: Mary Ballachino
Project editor: Julie Marsh

Library of Congress Cataloging-in-Publication Data is available on file.

ISBN 978-0-7627-8469-1

Printed in the United States of America

10 9 8 7 6 5 4 3 2 1

The identification, selection, and processing of any wild plant for use as food requires reasonable care and attention to details since, as indicated in the text, certain parts are wholly unsuitable for use and, in some instances, are even toxic. Because attempts to use any wild plants for food depend on various factors controllable only by the reader, the author and Globe Pequot Press assume no liability for personal accident, illness, or death related to these activities.

CONTENTS

ACKNOWLEDGMENTS

Feeling fortunate to have found this planet, I acknowledge it as my home and promise to keep it clean, tread lightly on its floor, and thank it daily for all blessings bestowed. I beg it to forgive my mistakes, ill manners, and careless recklessness. And when each of my given days is complete, I promise to sit quiet and listen to the earth sing, feel the air move, and revere all the green glory that is only found here.

But plants don't write, edit, lay out, and produce books. That job went to Jessica Haberman, Imee Curiel, Julie Marsh, Sheryl Kober, and the entire staff at GPP/FalconGuides. And yes, John Kit, who helped me find the elusive persimmon. Without your help, the plants described herein would not get their due. Your kind, patient, and trusting approach coaxed these words from me, and your insightful and imaginative creation forged them into a desirable and helpful tool for aspiring foragers. Thank you!

INTRODUCTION

Plants came first: They are the magic wand of God—with them, with the firmament that supports them, we are possible. We eat plants, or eat animals that eat plants; therefore from plant chemistry came our skin and bones, blood and muscle. They are our food and medicine. In addition, they provide all the natural beauty, ambience, and culinary delights of a good life. They are the stuff of gardens and arboretums, forests and prairies, and mountain trails, and personally they have given this average, ordinary man a lifetime of entertainment—such simple pleasures, all free and described in the pages that follow.

Read thoroughly the "Foraging Rules" listed below. Follow these instructions and memorize the poisonous plants listed in the appendix. Although this information does not guarantee immunity from allergic reactions, it does provide basic protection against potentially toxic mistakes. The "Forager's Dozen" chapter presents twelve of my favorite wild plant foods, most of which can be found from coast to coast. "Forager's Dozen Mushrooms" is a novel chapter, an introduction to twelve easy-to-identify mushrooms that will add hours of pleasure while hiking and numerous culinary delights for your table. "Yards, Gardens, Prairies, and Meadows" is a collection of edible weeds and edible wildflowers found coast to coast in these environments—many of the best edibles come from this collection. "Fruit and Berries," the next chapter, is a one-stop collection of fruiting vines, shrubs, and trees. If it's a fruit or berry you are looking at, go here. The "Wetlands" chapter covers edible plants found along streams and rivers, lakes, and ponds. "Edible Plants of Eastern Forested Areas" provides a clutch of flowering plants found typically in hardwood forests. "Trees and Nuts" is a coast-to-coast look at shrubs and trees that produce nuts. "Edible Wild Plants of the Mountain West" specifies plants found in the national parks and wilderness sanctuaries of Wyoming, Montana, Idaho, Utah, Oregon, and Washington. "Edible Plants of the Desert" describes food from extremely dry environments. And "Marine Vegetables" provides pictures and insights specific to edible marine and tidal area wild plant foods. Information on poisonous plants can be found in the appendix.

Read this book from cover to cover. Use it in the field and at home. Cross-check different chapters, as there are close relatives of several plants found in different environments. Start with the "Forager's Dozen," identify these plants, and then progress to the "Yards, Gardens, Prairies, and Meadows" chapter, which covers numerous familiar plants. As you forage through different environments, match the environment to its corresponding chapter and build your repertoire of wild foods.

Carry this book next to your heart or on your hip when venturing forth seeking delectable wild treasures to grace your table and serve to your friends. Many recipes are described here to excite you, but your unique personal discoveries will soon humble what I know. So think freely, my friend, invent and conceive—pass through this door of infinite possibilities and let your creative energy run wild.

WILD PLANT FORAGING RULES

1. It's a good idea to watch a plant through its growth cycle before eating it. This is helpful because many wild plants taste best just as they break through the ground, when they are small, furled, and difficult to identify. By watching them grow for a year, you will know what you are looking for in every season and where to find it.

2. Before eating any wild plants, study with an expert or take the plant to an expert for positive identification. Always cross-reference with two or more field guides. Make certain you have seen color photos of the plants; black-and-white photos or illustrations are not sufficient for positive identification.

3. After positive identification of an edible plant, taste only a very small amount of it. This precaution protects you from an allergic reaction or ill effects caused by misidentification.

4. Beware of the carrot family: Hemlock, water hemlock, and other members of this family are extremely poisono⸱ ⸱Le⸱⸱⸱⸱⸱ ⸱ distinguish hemlock and water hemlock from elder (elderberrie⸱

5. Practice conservation. Never collect more plants than you intend to u⸱⸱. Do not pick rare or endangered species. Work to restore wild plants from areas where they have disappeared. Do not plant alien or invasive species in your garden—check with your state's cooperative extension services for details.

6. Avoid harvesting plants from polluted ground. Plants growing along roads are tainted with benzene, lead, oil, and other auto pollutants. Plants dwelling in streams and along fields near farms are polluted with herbicides and pesticides. Forage carefully. Droppings from wild game may spread bacteria, viruses, worms, giardia, amoebas, and other forms of contamination into water that nurtures edible wild plants. Wash and cook all plants foraged from wild lands.

7. Purchase wild plants from seed and live-plant purveyors like Richter's and Pacific Botanicals (see Appendix C: References and Resources). Grow them in your garden, close to your kitchen. Make wild f⸱ ⸱ntegral part of your diet.

Forager's Dozen

Just outside the door, in the neighborhood, and in fields and forests nearby dwell the Forager's Dozen—twelve edible wild plants that are free and provide superior nutrition. What's more, they possess a variety of flavors that are delicious and satisfying. Find these twelve plants almost everywhere, from coast to coast and from mountains to marshes—à dozen plants that are easy to find, easy to prepare, and versatile—aggressive, open pollinated perennial plants you can move to your garden, putting at your fingertips the right stuff for a robust and healthy diet.

1. **STINGING NETTLE** is number one. Transfer several of these aggressive plants to your secret garden and reap immediate rewards. Simply pinch off the top whorl of leaves from each plant, wash them, then steam or sauté the leaves for about 2 minutes to vaporize the stinging chemistry. Use the blanched leaves as a pizza topping, in stews and soups, and on sandwiches. Add it to your favorite sauces. Stuff it inside a sausage. Stinging nettle is versatile and provides a distinctive flavor you will come back for again and again. Here's the bonus: When you pinch off that whorl of leaves, the plant bifurcates and doubles your harvest the next time around. Add this tasty, mineral-rich plant to your diet today.

2. **WILD LEEKS** come in numerous varieties: wild chives, wild garlic, wild leeks, and wild onions. My favorite is *Allium tricoccum,* the wild leek, or what mountain folks call ramps. Find leeks in shady areas, typically forests east of the Missouri River. Simplicity is best when preparing this plant. All of it is edible. Sauté in olive oil with a few drops of soy. Cook until tender; eat leaves and bulb. By June the aerial parts of the plant die off, and a flower spike with white florets leads you to the colony. Dig the bulbs and stuff them in olives. Purchase party stuffer olives, reheat the brine, stuff a leek in each olive, return to hot brine, and the jar seals. When leeks are not available, stuff olives with other varieties of the wild onion family. Use the leaves anywhere and everywhere: salads, martinis, pasta, sauces, sandwiches—you get the idea. More about this edible family later in the book.

3. **VIOLETS** (*Viola* spp.), found coast to coast in various hues, are great in any dish where color and taste are prerequisites. Leaves and flowers are edible. Transfer them to your garden, and let them compete with your pansies and tulip petals for space on the salad.

4. **WATERCRESS** is a pungent spicy green that adds zest and character to any dish. Cream it into soup, stuff it in a frittata, pump up an omelet, or put zip in a salad. Find a spring or free-flowing stream near you, prowl around, and reward your effort with this spicy, high-kicking, and versatile food.

5. **CATTAILS,** found near your watercress and leek source, have everything you need to survive—better yet, thrive. In June the flower heads are edible. Gather the male (top head), strip away the reproductive parts in quantity, and freeze. Use periodically to boost nutrition in pancakes, muffins, bread, pizzas, and all those other dishes and treats that require dough or batter. Steam the female heads like corn, add butter, and eat on the stick. Cattail roots and shoots are starch-rich, quick-energy food—best harvested in the fall or spring.

6. **DAYLILIES,** found coast to coast, harvested for their flower petals, impart a mild onion flavor to the palate. Use in salads or stir-fry. Harvest just the petals, however, and discard the reproductive parts, as they are bitter. The young shoots in spring are just OK, but give them a try—invent a surprising recipe.

7. **SUNFLOWERS** have edible seeds, and the flower petals, although tough, may be chopped into sauces, soups, eggs, and more. Jerusalem artichokes, the premier sunflower foodstuff, provide young edible shoots in spring, and the tubers of fall and spring are excellent. Cook tubers like potatoes, in every imaginable way. Sliced tubers make a starchy, flavorful base for a tortilla español. Yes! Go native, and use all these plants in your Mexican dishes.

8. **YELLOW WOOD SORREL,** often found in the yard or garden, is a lemony-tasting leprechaun. Eat both the small clover-like leaves and flowers. Best in salads, to balance the flavor of bitter greens, and fun to nibble while sprinkling the garden or hiking the fields.

9. **PURSLANE,** famous as a rich source of omega-3 fatty acids, volunteers in most gardens. Don't have any? Then mix in a bag of store-bought manure and stand back: Invariably manure holds the seeds that will pay off. Add purslane to salads; cook in soups, sauces, stews; and definitely eat it raw to get all of its nutritional benefits.

10. **DANDELION,** for many, is a noxious weed. OK, perhaps. But for me it helps in salads when an appetite-stimulating bitterness is required. Tear the leaves from the petiole (midrib vein) and add pieces judiciously to salads and cooked greens. Add flower petals to any salad where you want yellow to entice the imbibers.

11. **CHICKWEED** likes to compete with all the weeds wrestling for room along the edges of my lawn and neglected areas in the garden. A "green"-tasting herb with an edible flower bonus, it's available, ready, willing, and able—free nutrition, three or four steps from the kitchen, and a crunchy, tasty addition to the garden greens.

12. **BEEBALM** provides 2 edible flowers with contrasting flavors. *Monarda fistulosa* has a strong oregano flavor, enervating in tea, refreshing in Italian sauces, and delicately biting in Champagne. *Fistulosa*'s red-flowered sister, *Monarda didyma*, has florets that taste like pineapple nectar; use accordingly—on salads, in white wines. Also try it on cold soups and ice cream.

Beebalm, red didyma

Beebalm, blue fistulosa

Forager's Dozen Mushrooms

Mushroom foraging, like foraging for edible wild plants, is most rewarding, but few try it because of inadequate knowledge and a lack of experience fueled by fear. Here are a dozen mushrooms that are relatively easy to identify and safe to eat. These mushrooms offer variety and are available at different times throughout the year. The list is organized by ease of identification, availability, and season.

> *Caution: Like wild plants, there are dangerous mushrooms. I recommend you have at least three field guides (I have five) and key out any new or unknown mushroom in all three before eating it—even better, forage with a knowledgeable and experienced expert. Botanical gardens, state parks, and universities offer mycology (study of fungi) field trips.*

MORELS
Morchella spp.
Gray (yellow when mature) and black morels are often found about halfway down a slope in the woods, where spores have been washed and collected, usually in a tangle of brush. Dead ash, elm, apple, and tulip poplars are good places to look. West of the prairie region to the West Coast, find morels in burnouts, along the sides of trails, and along the edges of campgrounds. Use your food dryer to preserve these mushrooms if you are fortunate enough to get more than you can eat.

Food uses: Morels can be dried and stored, pickled, or simply rinsed and frozen whole. They are delicious in all dishes where mushrooms improve the taste: omelets, frittatas, pizza, pasta, burgers, veggie burgers (sauté with wild stinging nettle, asparagus, and red bell pepper). Sauté the first bunch of the season in a pinch of butter and olive oil. Dust with flour first, then sauté.

Black morels
These have a brain-like outer appearance, ridged and pitted, with pits arranged in columns, hollow in the middle, and a conical cap that tapers—2"–6" in height.

Habitat: Moist woods, under and around dead elms, hillsides under snags of dead logs, edges of trenches and runoff areas, fencerows of north-facing woods, burnout areas in the West. April and May in Michigan, later in the West.

Yellow morels

The yellow variety typically starts out gray and matures to yellow. Larger than black morels and with a full body of pits and ridges of different shapes and sizes, yellows appear a week or two later than blacks. They can exceed 10" in height but are typically in the 3"–6" range.

Habitat: Similar to black morels but will tolerate a little sun. Found on south-facing slopes in forests, campgrounds, streamsides of slow-moving streams, dank and moist places, April and May into June in Mountain West.

False morels

False morels are included here as a potentially toxic look-alike. I avoid this mushroom, although I have eaten it without ill effect. Others, however, find the mushroom toxic. False morels look similar to the edible morels but are strangely folded, as if nuked with radiation. They do not express the open hollow body of edible morels.

Habitat: Found in the same places as edible morels at the same time and even earlier.

DRYAD'S SADDLE

Polyporaceae (*Polyporus squamosus*)
I turn to this mushroom when morels are unavailable. Dryad's saddle is abundant, easy to identify, and available all year long. The flavor is not great, but it's good enough when thoroughly cooked and immersed in a soup or stew.

Identification: Forming shelves, this mushroom, often found in large clusters, is fan shaped, up to 15" in diameter, and pale tan to creamy yellow in color, with brown scales. This is a pored mushroom, with a tough stipe. Flesh is white, more tender near margins.

Habitat: Prefers wet woods and is best picked after a substantial rain (most tender then). Found in marshes; along streams; on dead timber, stumps, and dying trees of all kinds.

Food uses: Pick fresh young specimens that are wet and soft to the touch. A fresh *squamosus* releases a watermelon-like odor when torn. The mushroom gets tougher as you move toward the stem; use the outer tender edges. Eat fresh and cooked.

PUFFBALLS
Lycoperdales and Calvatia
(*Gasteromycetes* and *Lycoperdon*)

Identification: Puffballs range from small to large (1"–12" in diameter), whitish to brown (but not green, red, orange, or pink), oval to round or pear shaped; edible when fresh. Larger ones are easier to identify. They grow flat on top of the ground, without a distinctive stem. Be certain to slice the mushroom in half to check for gills or what may be the development of a gilled mushroom—a possible toxic amanita. Amanita gilled embryos emerge as adults from egg-shaped capsules; these capsules resemble a small puffball, but puffballs when sliced open do not present gills.

Eastern puffball

Western puffball

Habitat: Found on open ground under trees and shrubs and often in lawns. In Michigan we start seeing *Calvatia gigantea* in late August and September. Our favorite little brown puffball, found on dead maple and beech, appears at the same time. The small western variety, typically available in July (Montana), is found on open ground under pine trees and shrubs, often in lawns. *Lycoperdon perlatum* is found along forest roadsides and in driveways under pines from summer through fall.

Notes: Find puffballs of various species from coast to coast. Larger ones are easier to identify. Pick, cut open, and make certain the inside is white and not yellowing—and that there are no gills.

Food uses: I slice large puffballs thinly and dry them in a food dryer. Powder the end product, and add and stir in powder to cooking dishes (1 tablespoon to 1 quart broth) where you want to impart a mushroom flavor. Fresh mushrooms are breaded and sautéed or deep-fried. The flavor is good; the texture mushy.

OYSTER MUSHROOMS

Tricholomataceae (*Pleurotus ostreatus, Pleurotus pulmonarius*)

Oysters were abundant and free for the picking yesterday, Sunday, May 2, the earliest date we have ever found them. I found them on dead beech, poplar, ash, and maple. They will be available through December.

Identification: Oysters typically grow in large colonies and are gilled. Gills (lamellae) are the thin radiating blades beneath the cap of the mushroom, and with the oyster the gills are attached and run down the stem. Stem (stipe) is off to the side, supporting a funnel-like cap. *Pleurotus cornucopiae* is white to light gray in color, darkening to brown with age. *Pleurotus ostreatus* starts out white and ages to slate gray, then light brown. White- to pale-lilac-colored spores variable to lilac gray.

Habitat: Oyster mushrooms can be found on beech, maple, elm, oak, and birch. They grow in dense clusters—I once took a bushel off one downed beech. They will continue producing on the same tree or stump for several years, decomposing it—once the bark is gone, find a new tree.

Food uses: I prefer the taste of oyster mushrooms over morels. Pan-fry them battered in panko (Japanese bread crumbs). They're also great by themselves or with

Pan-seared buffalo steak with wild chives, onions, and oyster mushrooms

your favorite red or white oyster dip. They also can be used as a pizza topping, as well as in eggs, sauces, and Chinese and Mexican dishes.

KING BOLETE
Boletaceae (*Boletus edulis*)

Boletes are putrescent and break down into a slimy, mushy, odorous mass after sitting too long unrefrigerated. They carry a good deal of water, so don't wash before cooking—dry-brush but do not bathe.

Identification: 3"–10" in diameter, a bun-shaped mushroom with a moist, smooth, and viscous surface (like a browned hamburger bun). Color variable from biscuit brown, margins paler. Flesh is thick, often infested with worms, insects, and larvae. Tubes instead of gills, with the tube ends appearing to be stuffed with pith, first white in color and turning yellow, olive, to olive yellow as it ages—solitary and scattered and occasionally in groups of 2 or 3.

Warning: Avoid boletes with red or orange pores (tubes) and ones where cap surfaces or pores turn blue when bruised, as these may contain muscarine toxin. Avoid orange- and red-capped bolete look-alikes. Also avoid boletes with yellow pore surfaces that turn blue when bruised. And avoid orange-capped boletes altogether.

Habitat: I find king boletes in and around Yellowstone National Park in late July, typically in recovering burn areas, with 3"–10" spruce and pine new growth, and much dead timber on the ground. Farther west, in Montana, I stumble over them in campgrounds and along the edges of streams around the first and second weeks of August. I found several in one day during a warm year on Glacier Creek Trail in the Swan Valley, near Condon, Montana.

Food uses: The mushroom is watery—slice it thin and sauté. I cook them crisp. Cook into dishes and then freeze. It is too moist to dry. Eat and prepare as soon as possible, as its shelf life is short.

CHICKEN MUSHROOM
Polyporaceae (*Laetiporus sulphureus*)

Find one of these large mushrooms and you'll have food for days, if not weeks. Often found in vacant woodlots and near populated areas. No need to hike into the wilderness for this mushroom—it's easily seen from the road and often along roadsides clinging to trees.

Identification: A lemon to orange-yellow (darkening with age) bracket fungus, grows on trees, and typically grows in a semicircle, taking the shape of a convoluted fan; has softly rounded edges, tubes are yellow, and when fresh a slight squeeze will exude yellow juice. Smell is pungent.

Habitat: Grows on trees, typically oaks, but also willow, cherry, and yew—seasonally available from late spring until early fall. In Michigan they are available from June through September.

Food uses: This is a chewy, juicy mushroom that requires cleaning. Pull apart segments (layers), brush, and wash (I use a hose). Blanching removes any bitter taste. Texture and flavor when cooked is like chicken. I sauté the mushroom to cook and remove moisture, then freeze, then thaw later to use in stews, soups, pizza, and omelets. Ideal for vegetarians. Goes well in risotto and with curry and various homemade salsas.

HEN OF THE WOODS

Polyporaceae (*Grifola frondosa, Polyporus frondosus*)

Notes: Jill, my wife, found a 35-pound hen-of-the-woods mushroom in her secret place two years in a row.

Identification: Grows at the base of trees. Central section of branched stems terminates in individual caps. Grayish caps 1"–3" across, with wrinkled edges. Stems gray also; mushroom browns with age. Tubes instead of gills.

Habitat: Grows on trunks of dead and living trees and occasionally on stumps. Typically on oaks but found on other deciduous trees. Found in late August, September, and October in the northern tier of eastern states.

Food uses: Requires diligent cleaning, with many cracks and crevices containing dirt and an occasional creature. I use a hose. This tasty mushroom requires enough cooking to soften its sometimes tough texture (depending on freshness). It goes well in all mushroom dishes. It dries well for storage, but I like to cook it first in a dish and freeze it for later use.

WOOD EARS

Tremellales (*Auricularia auricula*)
I found these the first time while searching for morels—they were growing on small lengths of rotting wood. Found them throughout the summer; best after a soaking rain.

Identification: Rubbery fruiting body that resembles an ear; 1"–3" across. Has a jellylike texture and snaps in the mouth like rubber bands. It is tan brown with grayish hairs on the velvety inner surface. Stretch the mushroom to make certain it is elastic and rubbery. It produces white spores, and the surface, as mentioned, is rubbery.

Habitat: Woods, fringes of woods; grows on wood (extremely rotted wood)—wood that can be shredded with your fingers. Many sources mention elder trees as a preferred habitat. Although available for several months, I find it rarely, and often in unlikely mushroom habitats.

Food uses: Wash thoroughly, then add to Oriental stir-fries, or simply sautée in butter. Interesting chewy texture and surprisingly good taste that holds up either dried or frozen in cooked dishes. Great in sauces: Cook with wild leeks, thicken with sour cream, and serve over toast.

HONEY MUSHROOM

Tricholomataceae (*Armillaria mellea*)
In late summer and early fall, honey mushrooms appear in large numbers around the base of trees, stumps, and occasionally in the lawn, living off a submerged root. This is a destructive parasitic fungus that destroys many trees before their time.

Identification: Cap size ranges from ¾" to 8"; color varies from honey-like to dark brown, clearly visible yellow cottony ring; stem varies from 2" to 6" and is tough and fibrous (usually not eaten); gills vary from off-white to dark brown. Flesh is white with strong, sweet odor. Stem base is fused, and there is almost always a cluster of tiny scales at the cap's center. Found in large clumps, dispersing pale-cream, smooth elliptical spores—do a spore print to be certain this is the right mushroom. Choose carefully, as there are nasty look-alikes.

Habitat: Found in both deciduous and coniferous forests, on living or dead trees, stumps, and buried roots. Found from early summer to early winter and may reappear at same location in consecutive years, and occasionally in the same year.

Food uses: Boil caps for 2 minutes in slightly salted water, discard water, then use mushroom cap. Sauté, cook in sauces, thicken in cream seasoned with garlic and fresh basil. Cook into recipes and store in freezer. Drying toughens the mushroom, and it does not reconstitute easily.

LION'S MANE

Echinodontium (*Hericium erinaceus*)
This mushroom, always a surprise, is found inside a hollow log or hanging from a tree or stump. Various species are found in the western, eastern, and southern states.

Identification: 2"–20" across; a white, spiny mushroom that yellows with age. Dangling white spines give this fungus its common name. Spines may up to 1½" long and give the fungus the appearance of a lion's mane. Spore print is white. Fungoid attached to tree with a thick and solid white base—available in late summer and throughout the fall.

Habitat: Found singly and occasionally in pairs on the same wound from a deciduous tree (hardwood). You may have to climb to harvest. Mature and old-growth woods are productive.

Food uses: A delicious mushroom sautéed and eaten by itself or served hot in a vegetarian sandwich. Store prepared dishes in your freezer. Soften mushroom by cooking, which also eliminates some of the water from these hydrated specimens. Goes well with lemony marinades.

Yards, Gardens, Prairies, and Meadows

AMARANTH

Amaranth (*Amaranthus* spp.)

Identification: Amaranth, sometimes referred to as red root, is a hairy, stout weed with ovate to lance-shaped leaves on long stalks, and flowers in dense clusters on an elongated stem, bristly. Seeds typically black. Plant flowers in July and August, and seeds are available soon after.

Habitat: Roadsides, fields, waste ground east and west of the Mississippi River at lower elevations.

Food uses: Young shoots and leaves eaten raw or cooked. May be dried and reconstituted in hot water for winter food. Seeds used whole as cooked cereal. Seeds ground into flour and used to supplement flour for bread, muffins, etc. Seeds also added whole to bread, pancakes, and waffles. *Pinole* (*atole*) is a hot corn drink made with toasted amaranth seeds and roasted blue or white cornmeal. Spread cornmeal and amaranth seeds on a cookie sheet or aluminum foil. Toast in 425°F oven for 8–10 minutes. Add sugar and cinnamon, stir into hot milk, and simmer for 15 minutes. Native Americans ate leaves and seeds mixed with grease and cooked. Try a mixed-greens dish of young and tender amaranth leaves combined with mustard, plantain, dock, and nettle and cooked with bacon.

Medicinal uses: Native Americans used this plant mixed with green corn in sacred rituals. Leaves are astringent and used to stem profuse menstruation.

ASIATIC DAYFLOWER

Commelinaceae (*Commelina communis*)

Identification: Common weed in many gardens. Erect stems collapse on themselves as they grow (up to 3'). Deep-blue flowers, ½"–¾" wide, 2 rounded petals (like Mickey Mouse ears) with a small white petal behind the pair. Flower's ovary sheathed in 3

green sepals; 6 yellow-tipped stamens. Fleshy, oblong leaves, 3"–5" long, pointed tips. Leaves sheath stem.

Habitat: Found nationwide in gardens and on roadsides. Alien weed: originated in China.

Food uses: This free food comes up late every year. Young leaves and shoots can be added to salads. I get so many of these plants in my garden that I pull whole shoots, wash them, and add them to stir-fries. Entire flower is edible. As fruit matures, the seed capsule (tucked in the sepal sheath) is a crunchy treat. In late summer flowers keep coming. You can eat seedpods for a healthful dose of essential oils and phytosterols.

Medicinal uses: In China, leaf tea is used as a sore-throat gargle and for urinary tract infections, acute intestinal enteritis, and dysentery. Tea is also used to reduce fevers, as a detoxicant, and as a diuretic (to treat edema from joint swelling and pain from arthritis). Flowers contain isoflavones and phytosterols. Seeds contain fatty acids and essential and nonessential amino acids.

BURDOCK, GOBO BURDOCK
Compositae (*Arctium lappa*)

Identification: Biennial, first year's growth sprouts broad elephant ear–like leaves (heart shaped) that grow directly from a deep taproot. Second-year leaves are slightly smaller; mature plant is many branched and spreading to 7' or 8', although often much smaller. Flowers are crimson with inward-curving bracts that eventually form the mature seed capsule, which is a burr. This is the plant that deposits burrs on your dog and your trousers. Break open the seed capsule, and plant the seeds.

Habitat: Found in the Northern Hemisphere, temperate zone. Found in gardens, along roadsides, and just about every place you walk your dog, providing an entertaining burr-pulling party. My favorite site is a lowland marsh with rich muck that produces outstanding specimens.

Food uses: Harvest roots in autumn or spring of the first year's growth. Root may be 20" or longer. Peel the root, wash, slice diagonally (julienne), and stir-fry, steam, or sauté. First year's leaves may be peeled, cooked, and eaten. Slivered roots taste great on pizza for texture and flavor. Second-year flower spikes cut and peeled—sauté or steam.

Medicinal uses: Historically used to treat immune system deficiency and skin conditions. Leaf infusion (tea) used for chronic skin problems. Root oil used the same way: Soak the chopped root in olive oil in the refrigerator for 1 month. Root as food considered antidiabetic, regulating blood sugar when lightly cooked. Root tea and eating the root reported to treat acne. Root polysaccharides said to lower blood sugar; polysaccharides require more steps in digestion, thus the release of glucose is slow and gradual. According to a Japanese study, the root is anti-mutagenic (anticancer) in animal studies.

Warning: Avoid if pregnant or lactating.

Notes: The root, called *gobo* in Asian markets, sells for as much as $8 a pound. It's free if in your backyard, so put it there. Pull burrs off a dog or your trousers, crush burrs to release seeds, spread seeds on scuffed soil in November. Plant thickly, and then thin seedlings in May.

CHICORY

Compositae (*Cichorium intybus*)
An attractive garden flower with edible leaves, edible flowers, and a digestion-stimulating root.

Identification: Biennial or perennial to 4'; stem is erect, with few branches. Lanceolate (lance-shaped) leaves in a basal whorl, as well as additional smaller upper leaves on stem. Blue flowers (rarely white or pink) with square-tipped rays, and a dandelion-like root. Plant blooms July through September.

Habitat: Conspicuous flowers along roadsides, disturbed areas, fields, meadows, waste ground nationwide.

Food uses: The root can be dried, roasted, mixed with coffee beans, then ground to yield Cajun coffee. The flower petals are slightly bitter and add a nice contrast when stirred into cottage cheese (let the blossoms infuse into the cheese overnight in the refrigerator). The slightly bitter flowers are a healthful addition to salads, jump-starting the digestion process. Tasty flower, bitter root.

Medicinal uses: Root dried or fresh is decocted in water as a diuretic, dietetic, and laxative. Root tea stimulates digestion, improving peristalsis and absorption. Root decoction used externally to treat fever blisters. Cherokee used root infusion as a nervine—a tonic for the nerves. Homeopathic preparation used for gallbladder and liver complaints. Root decoction may reduce blood sugar. Root constituents are antibacterial in vitro. Animal studies show chicory extract slows heart rate.

Warning: A few sources suggest long-term excessive use of chicory may impair vision. This has not been scientifically proven.

CLOVER, RED

Fabaceae (*Trifolium pratense*)
Identification: Often 3 leaflets showing pale chevron; round flower head; rose-purple flower petals.

Habitat: Common roadside companion throughout the United States.

Food uses: Petals can be batter-fried or eaten raw in salads. Whole aerial parts of plant can be infused to make a bland but healthful tea.

Medicinal uses: Tea from flowers is flavonoid rich, providing antioxidant, anticancer protection. Skilled herbalists used this plant to treat cuts, burns, and liver ailments. Integral part of the Essiac anticancer formula consisting of burdock root, slippery elm bark, rhubarb root, watercress, sheep sorrel, blessed thistle, red clover, and kelp.

DANDELION

Compositae (*Taraxacum officinale*)
Identification: Basal whorl of toothed leaves. Yellow flower with numerous rays. Torn leaf and/or flower stem will exude white-colored latex.

Habitat: Common yard bounty. Found in temperate regions worldwide.

Food uses: No waste—eat flower, root, leaves, and crown. A vitamin- and mineral-rich salad green. Tear it into small pieces for salad, mix with thyme and fennel, nasturtiums, along with other salad ingredients. Thyme and fennel balance the bitterness of dandelions. Make a mineral-rich tea from the roots and leaves. Gently simmer chopped fresh roots for a stomach bitters. Cook fresh leaves early in season with olive oil, bacon, and lemon juice. As season progresses leaves become bitter: Pour copious

amount of water on the late-summer plants—the morning harvest will be sweeter. Even when bitter, leaves are a healthy addition to stir-fry. Try with tofu. Cook in oyster oil, with cayenne, garlic, and beef strips. Simmer or sauté with leeks, kale, and turnip greens.

Medicinal uses: Dried leaves and autumn roots are infused or decocted as a liver-cleansing tonic, aiding digestion and cleansing the blood. It is a diuretic, traditionally used to treat PMS, having a mild laxative effect, and may relieve inflammation and congestion of gallbladder and liver. Native Americans applied steamed leaves externally (poultice) to stomachaches. Eating green leaves considered a tonic and blood purifier, root taken to increase lactation and as a mild laxative and for dyspepsia. The bitter taste of dandelion is an appetite stimulant and may be helpful in treating anorexia. Because the bitter dandelion root decoction raises HCL in stomach, it improves calcium breakdown and absorption, increasing bile production and therefore lowering capacity (1 bile molecule requires 2 cholesterol molecules from the liver).

DAYLILY
Liliaceae (*Hemerocallis fulva*)

Identification: Yellow, tuberous roots; long, narrow, lance-like leaves; orange lily flower. Found along roadsides; transplant to clean soil away from auto pollution.

Habitat: Throughout the United States. Shade and sun tolerant; excellent garden transplant.

Food uses: Onion-tasting flowers are flavonoid rich. Daylily petals teased apart from the whole flower and tossed in with salad greens. Flowers (without pistils and stamens) and unopened buds can be stir-fried or batter-dipped and cooked tempura-style. Try the sautéed flowers wrapped in wontons, steamed. Wrap buds and flowers in a wonton, dip in soy and mustard—delicious. Buds can also be steamed, boiled, or deep-fried, and then served with butter or cheese sauce. Firm root tubers harvested all year. Add raw to salads or cook like a potato.

Note: I eat just the flower petals, not the reproductive organs, as the stamen, pistils, anthers, and filaments are bitter.

Medicinal uses: Daylily buds contain more protein and vitamin C than green beans and asparagus. Traditional people used the extract of the herb to treat cancer.

There is evidence that extracts of daylily roots and crowns are pain relievers, a diuretic, and an antidote to arsenic poisoning. Daylily flowers are known to possess antioxidant properties and cyclooxygenase (COX) inhibitory; inhibition of COX can provide relief from the symptoms of inflammation and pain.

Warning: Use plant only when in bloom. Early growth resembles poisonous iris shoots (see Appendix A: Poisonous Plants); daylily's yellowish tubers are distinctive.

EVENING PRIMROSE
Onagraceae (*Oenothera biennis*)

Identification: Biennial that grows to 3' or more with fleshy turnip-like root. First-year plant is a basal rosette of leaves, second year is erect plant, conspicuous in the fall with its large seed-filled fruit capsules. Oblong lance-shaped leaves, pointed and finely dentate. Fragrant bugle-shaped yellow flowers are 1" long and grow from the leaf axils. Flowers open in evening and have 4 petals, 4 sepals, and 8 stamens. Fruit is linear-oblong, 4 sided, downy, about ½"–1" in length, producing seeds that are dark gray to black with sharp edges. Western varieties have white-, yellow-, or pink-colored flowers.

Habitat: Found in gardens, along roadsides, on waste ground, fields, and prairies up and down and across North America. More than 20 species inhabit the western states.

Food uses: The root is edible (biennial plant: first-year root best, in the fall or early spring of second year). New leaves of first or second year are edible in salads and stir-fry. The leaves are tough and need to be cooked. Seeds poured from seed capsule (seed capsule looks like small, dried okra pod). Immature seed capsules may be cooked like okra but don't taste like okra—nothing like okra, not worth the trouble. But primrose seeds are available on cross-country ski trips throughout the winter. I pour them from the capsule and eat out of hand.

Medicinal uses: Seed oil is used to treat essential fatty acid deficiency and to lower cholesterol. Cholesterol-lowering effect proved successful in a double-blind crossover study conducted in 1996. Native Americans used warm root poultice to treat piles. Roots chewed to increase strength and endurance. Whole plant bruised, soaked, and used as a poultice on bruises and sores. Seed extract said to dilate coronary arteries and clear arterial obstruction.

GOATSBEARD OYSTER PLANT, YELLOW

Asteraceae (*Tragopogon dubius*)
Identification: Looks like a large dandelion; grows 2'–4' tall, with a smooth stem with yellow flower head. Stem hollow just below flower head, yellow rayed flower, 2½" in diameter, bladelike leaves; entire plant grows to 3', typically less.

Habitat: Dry areas, fields, open fringes of woods, fence lines, meadows, and burnouts. Found nationwide from east to west, north into Ontario and south to Texas.

Food uses: Young leaves boiled or sautéed. I have eaten flower petals, but do so judiciously, as I appear to be the only author who does.

Medicinal uses: Native Americans made a cold infusion of whole plant to treat animal bites and used latex sap as a milk substitute. Latex will dry and may be chewed; cathartic.

HEAL ALL, SELFHEAL

Lamiaceae (*Prunella vulgaris*)
Identification: Blue to violet bract of flowers clustered in a whorl at the end of the square stem. Stem, when young, is erect and may fall and creep. Plants are typically 6"–10" in height. Leaves ovate to lance shaped, margins are dentate to entire, and opposite.

Habitat: Found on waste ground, lawns, fields, and margins of woods nationwide.

Food uses: Sauté small leaves with stinging nettle and add to soups. Aerial parts made into an infusion with mint leaves and a twist of lime.

Medicinal uses: Documented use by the Chinese for more than 2,200 years, self-heal used for liver complaints and improving the function of the liver. The whole plant used in infusion to stimulate the liver and gallbladder and promote healing—considered alterative, and capable of changing the course of a chronic disease.

HOPS

Cannabaceae (*Humulus lupulus*)

Identification: A perennial climbing vine with pencil-thick stems that do not turn woody. The plant climbs through shrubs. Leaves are opposite, 3–5 lobed, and serrated. Male flowers are small, inconspicuous, and yellowish green. Female flowers have numerous florets, and a fruit cone grows from the flowers. Cone may be yellowish to gray depending on whether it is fresh or dried. The scales of the cone contain the bitter drug used in beer and digestive teas.

Habitat: It has escaped from cultivation and is found in marshes, meadows, and the edges of woods. Cultivated stands can be seen in Washington State, east of Seattle in the Yakima Valley, and in Idaho along the Canadian border.

Food uses: The fruit cone (gray to yellow) used in the production of beer; gives it a bitter flavor. The more hops, the greater the bitterness, as in Pilsner Urquell and popular IPA brews. Also used as a sedative tea. Cone-like flowers are placed in pillows to improve sleep.

Warning: Contact with pollen has caused allergic reactions.

Medicinal uses: Infusion of the flower or seed cone is emollient, sedative, and a bitter digestive stimulant. Native Americans used it in sweat lodges by soaking leaves and throwing the flowers on hot rocks. Basque shepherds use the cones in infusion as a calming sedative and digestive. They drink the tea to settle jittered nerves and stimulate digestive juices to hasten peristalsis and catharsis. Pioneers and Native Americans also used the tea to treat fevers from acute infections. Research suggests that the flower tea may impart estrogenic effect. Although subsequent research has not shown this effect, it is a phytoestrogen.

Notes: According to a few sources, smoking hops like marijuana may provide a mild sedative effect; the 2 species are related. To make a sleep aid, add about 1 teaspoon of dried flowers to a 6-ounce cup of hot water, just off the boil. Cover and let cool to lukewarm, then drink.

JERUSALEM ARTICHOKE, SUN CHOKE

Asteraceae (*Helianthus tuberosus*)
Identification: Yellow sunflower; broad ovate, rough leaves, lower leaves opposite, upper leaves alternate; hairy stem; tuberous root.

Habitat: Throughout the United States, along roadsides, gardens, fields.

Food uses: Tuber peeled, sliced, and eaten raw, and has taste similar to water chestnut. Also microwave, bake, or boil like a potato. This plant is worth looking for. I like it as a base for a tortilla española (frittata). Spread them on the bottom of an iron skillet, pour over 6 whipped eggs, add other wild plants (chopped), sharp cheese (grated); cook at 375°F for 15 minutes, serve.

Note: Add tubers to your garden and they'll provide a substantial food source that continues to reproduce year after year. Harvest tubers in fall and spring.

Medicinal uses: Tea made from flowers and leaves is a traditional treatment for arthritis. Inulin-rich tuber is slow to release sugars, making it a good food for diabetics.

LAMB'S QUARTER, PIGWEED, GOOSEFOOT

Chenopodiaceae (*Chenopodium album*)
Identification: To 5' in height, with light-green (grayish green) leaves with powderlike substance beneath, coarsely toothed, with a goosefoot or diamond shape. Small green flowers are in clusters, growing from top third of plant and many of the branches. Seeds are gray colored.

Habitat: Across the nation in meadows, along roadsides, gardens, waste ground, edges of cultivated fields.

Food uses: Add lamb's quarter leaves to salads, stir-fry, and steamed wontons with quinoa, carrots, burdock root. Roll wontons in quinoa seeds before steaming. Seeds may be ground and used in baking recipes. The herb flavors corn and fish dishes and Mexican foods. Add seeds to pancakes and waffles, bread, pizza dough. Also great as a cooked cereal and best when part of a multigrain cereal. Cook it like rice.

Medicinal uses: Lamb's quarter tea used for stomachache, scurvy, diarrhea. Also poultice over wounds and bites. In Mexico, cooked leaves and seed heads are believed to keep the digestive system clean and healthy. Cree used leaves for arthritis, rheumatism—washing joints and limbs with the decoction. Inuit people believe the leaves, when cooked with beans, dispel gas. Iroquois used a cold infusion of the plant to treat diarrhea. Leaves are high in vitamin C content (used to treat scurvy), and when eaten with seeds, the essential amino acid content is complete.

MILKWEED, COMMON MILKWEED
Asclepiadaceae (*Asclepias syriaca*)

Identification: Perennial to 4' with a single stem, leaves opposite, large, elliptical to 8" in length. Pink flowers in drooping clusters grow from leaf axils. Seedpod is striking, Arabian slipper–like.

Habitat: Edges of cornfields, waste ground, roadsides, railroad rights-of-way, meadows, dune lands, desert, gardens. Various species found nationwide.

Food uses: Native Americans prepared *Asclepias syriaca* like asparagus before milky sap appears (cooked in 2 changes of water). Flower buds are prepared like cooked broccoli when harvested before they open. Flowers buds and seedpods are prepared as follows: Boil water, pour over seedpods, let water and pods steep for 5 minutes, then pour off water. Repeat, pour a second boil of water over once-steeped pods, pour off water, and then stir-fry in olive oil or butter. Many people use 3 water baths over pods—recommended for first encounters. Flowers may be dried and stored for winter use in soups, stew. Keep in mind I have only eaten *A. syriaca*. Other species may be toxic. Do not experiment unless guided by an expert.

> *Warning: Plant parts contain a cardiac glycoside that must be denatured by repetitive cooking. First-time users, eat a very small bite of the plant to see if you have a reaction. Many people eat the plant, so it is contained here, but not without warning.*

Medicinal uses: Native Americans pounded or split the roots to expose their flesh for drying. Dried roots in decoction have a mild cardiac-stimulating effect—without the toxic effects of digitalis. Be warned: This should be practiced with medical supervision because *A. syriaca* contains toxic cardiac glycosides and requires careful preparation before use. Native Americans believed the plant was a lactagogue because of the milky white sap, per the Doctrine of Signatures, or "like treats like." Latex from leaves rubbed on warts and applied over insect stings, bites, and spider envenomations. According to Duke and Foster in *Peterson's Field Guide to Medicinal*

Plants (p. 154), the plant is considered "dangerous and contraceptive"—respect this, and use the plant judiciously.

Warning: Root decoction emetic; may stimulate the heart; some people may experience allergic reactions to the milky sap.

PLANTAIN

Plantaginaceae (*Plantago lanceolata; P. major; P. maritima*)

Identification: Several varieties are found across the United States. The difference is in the leaves: *P. major*'s leaves are broad and ovate, and *P. lanceolata*'s leaves are narrow and lance shaped. *Plantago maritima*'s leaves are narrower, almost linear, and it is found along the West Coast, often submerged during high tide. The green flowers of all 3 are born on terminal spikes.

Habitat: Discover these common plants on open ground, wasteland, edges of fields and roads, and lawns nationwide. *Plantago maritima,* as mentioned, is found in the upper tidal zone.

Food uses: In the spring I pluck whole leaves from my garden and yard, chop them into salads, or sauté them with wild leeks, nettles, dandelions, and watercress. Cut summer and autumn leaves from the tough midleaf vein (rib) before adding to salads. Seeds added to baked goods to improve fiber load.

Medicinal uses: Strip off flowering heads between thumb and forefinger into hot water to form mucilaginous drink for treating constipation. Crushed plant applied to dermatitis to treat poison ivy. Native Americans chewed the leaves, mixing in saliva and defensin (antibiotic in our mouths) to provide an antiseptic and immune-stimulating poultice to be applied to wounds, scrapes, cuts, and bruises. It is styptic, stopping blood flow. Tea is diuretic, decongestant, expectorant, and may be helpful in diarrhea, dysentery, irritable bowel syndrome, laryngitis, and urinary tract bleeding. Acubin in plantain increases uric acid excretion by kidneys and may be helpful in treating gout. *P. lanceolata* extract from the fresh plant may fight colds (4 grams of herb to 1 cup boiling water), may alleviate symptoms of bronchitis and cough, and may reduce fever. It is German Commission E–approved for treating inflammation of pharynx and mouth, and for skin inflammations. Typically, a dose is 3–6 grams of the fresh whole herb (aerial parts when in bloom) added to a cup of water just off the boil. Let cool, then drink; taken 3 or 4 times a day.

POKEWEED, POKE SALAD
Phytolaccaceae (*Phytolacca americana*)

Identification: A smooth-skinned plant with purple stems when mature, to 10' tall but more typically 5'. Stems are hollow and usually marked with grooves. The root is long and thick. Leaves are ovate-lanceolate, alternate, 5"–10" in length, with entire margins. When rubbed, leaves provide a musty indicative scent. Flowers are on racemes, with a calyx but no corolla. Berries are purplish to black when ripe.

Habitat: From the Missouri River east to the coast and south to the Gulf. Found on waste ground, fields, roadsides, gardens.

Food uses: The young shoots of this plant are edible in the spring. Leaves are boiled in 2 changes of water. Avoid poke once the stem and leaf petioles have turned purple. The lectin content rises as the plant matures. Cooking destroys some of the lectins, and digestive juices get others. Your window of opportunity is short. This is an excellent tasting green. If you are not certain, you can find these greens canned and commercially available.

Medicinal uses: Native Americans traditionally used the root poultice over rheumatoid joints. Berries made into tea for rheumatic conditions. Berry tea is also used to treat dysentery. Infusion of root used for eczema, ulcerated wounds, and to reduce swelling. Dried and powdered roots spread over cuts and sores. Plant used as a proven laxative and emetic. A leaf decoction mixed with other plants taken as a blood purifier and stimulant. Infusion of root and branches used in sweat lodges to produce steam, considered antirheumatic. Root pounded and mixed with grease and applied to bunions.

PURSLANE
Portulacaceae (*Portulaca oleracea*)

Identification: Spreading succulent that sprawls through garden with thick, fleshy, shiny ovate leaves. Stems are many branched, supporting small inconspicuous flowers.

Habitat: Gardens and waste ground, even cracks in the sidewalk, from coast to coast. Volunteers sprout from composted manure.

Food uses: Purslane is a common garden plant, an alien creeper with ovate leaves, thick and succulent—eaten right off the ground, put in salads, and chopped into soup. The payoff is omega-3 essential fatty acids. Native Americans ate the leaves as a raw or cooked vegetable. It was also boiled in soups and with meats. Try it chopped in salads or in salad dressing, even turkey stuffing. Native Americans ate purslane raw with meat and green chiles. Can be dried and reconstituted as a winter food. Cow manure (store bought) put on the garden invariably produces purslane.

Medicinal uses: Crush plant and apply as a poultice or skin lotion. Whole plant in decoction is used to treat worms. Juice used to treat earaches. Juice of whole plant considered a tonic. Used in the past as an antidote to unspecified herbal toxins. Infusion of leaf stems used to stem diarrhea. Mashed plant used as a poultice over burns and bruises. Decoction of whole plant considered an antiseptic wash and was eaten as a traditional remedy to treat stomachache. Essential fatty acids may help prevent inflammatory conditions such as heart disease, diabetes, and arthritis.

SPIDERWORT, WIDOW'S TEARS, SPIDER PLANT
Commelinaceae (*Tradescantia virginiana, T. occidentalis, T. pinetorum*)

Identification: Leaves are long, tough, swordlike, smooth, with entire margins. Numerous leaves grow from the base (no stem). Flowers are orchidlike, in drooping terminal clusters, deep blue; open in the morning and closed by afternoon. The plant blooms continuously throughout summer. There are at least 4 species in North America.

Habitat: In my garden and along railroad rights-of-way, roadsides, fields, and prairies from coast to coast.

Food uses: Tender shoots of spring eaten raw or cooked. Flowers are edible throughout year; pick in morning before they wilt. Try them in salads, stir-fry, or right off the plant. Flowers dipped in egg white and coated with powdered sugar. Flowers are mucilaginous.

Medicinal uses: Root tea was used as a laxative and for female kidney disorders and stomach problems. Crushed and smashed aerial parts of plant used as a poultice over insect bites, stings, and to bind wounds. Aerial infusion is also used to treat stomachache. Native Americans and pioneers used the crushed plant as a poultice to treat cancer. *T. occidentalis* tea used as a diuretic, and infused plant said to be an aphrodisiac.

Mixteca tribe of Mexico bound Hernan Cortez's thigh wound with this plant and is credited for saving his life. As a garden perennial, this plant gives and gives and gives.

THISTLE, BULL
Onagraceae (*Cirsium vulgare*)

Identification: Thorny biennial; ¾" purple flower with numerous rays rises from spiny bract. Barbed, deeply cut leaves of the first year's growth eaten after the spines are stripped away with a knife—wear gloves when harvesting roots and leaves.

Habitat: Coast to coast in northern-tier states, mountainsides, streamsides, waste ground, roadsides, dry, well-drained areas.

Food uses: Use a knife to strip thorny armor away from leaves. Eat raw or cooked; flavor similar to celery. Harvest leaves in the spring and fall. In summer flower petals sprinkled over salads. Roots can be boiled, sliced, and stir-fried. Some folks steam outer green bract around flower heads and eat it like an artichoke.

Medicinal uses: The Chinese use thistle teas and decoctions to treat appendicitis, internal bleeding, and inflammations.

WILD GARLIC
Liliaceae (*Allium sativum*)

Identification: Long, narrow, pencil-like leaf stalk; flower head bears small green plantlets that drop off and propagate.

Habitat: Throughout the United States in fields, vacant lots, railroad sides, and other disturbed land.

Food uses: Always cook wild garlic and wild onions to cleave inulin molecules to a digestible sugar. Inulin is a polysaccharide, a stored-energy source typically found in roots and tubers and not easily digested. Taste a few bulbs in the spring, then eat the florets all summer.

Medicinal uses: Wild garlic, chives, and onions may reduce blood pressure, lower cholesterol, lower blood sugar, and protect you from acute infections such as a cold or the flu.

WILD ONIONS, CHIVES
Liliaceae (*Allium* spp.)

Identification: Like wild garlic, onions and chives come early. Chives are some of the first flowers of spring, and they shoot up as tender rounded stems to 18" tall. Garlic leaves are flattened; chives and onions are round.

Habitat: Disturbed ground, roadsides, fringes of lawns, fields, and meadows nationwide.

Food uses: Wild onion, field onions, wild chives, wild garlic, and wild leeks have edible flowers and edible bulbs. It is a good idea to cook the wild onion bulbs, as the inulin content is difficult for some people to digest. Cooking will break down this polysaccharide to a more manageable chain. After flowers bloom on these *Allium* species, a little bulblet, which is very edible, forms on the flower head. Pickle or stir-fry with vegetables and pork.

Medicinal uses: Like the cultivars onions, garlic, and leeks, wild alliums are infection fighters and may lower blood pressure. Sulfur compounds in alliums protect from acute infections like colds and flu. Like wild garlic, chives and onions reduce blood pressure, lower cholesterol, and stabilize or lower blood sugar.

WINTER CRESS AND BLACK MUSTARD

Brassicaceae (*Barbarea vulgaris, Brassica nigra*)

Identification: Both herbs are peppery tasting and have yellow flowers, with black mustard being preferred. Both have 4-petaled flowers, with black mustard flowers to ½" and winter cress to ⅓". Lower leaves of both plants divided into 5 segments (lobes), on winter cress with 4 lateral lobes and 1 terminal lobe; upper leaves on winter cress clasp stem, whereas upper leaves on black mustard are lance shaped and toothed and not lobed.

Habitat: Fields, pastures, roadsides, and wetland edges nationwide.

Food uses: Eat the flowers and leaves. Allow a few flowers to go to seed for next year's crop. Greens come early, in March and April. Flowers are best early: April for winter cress, June for black mustard. Black mustard is a pleasant addition to salad and cooked greens.

Black mustard

Medicinal uses: Plants have isothiocyanates hydrolyzed to sulforaphane in the mouth to provide protection from cancer.

Fruit and Berries

APPLE
Malvaceae (*Malus domestica*)

Identification: Tree, cultivated and escaped to the wild, blossoms white to pink; 35' tall, with alternate ovate leaves, finely serrated.

Habitat: Originally from central Asia temperate region, widely cultivated in America and has escaped to the wild. Found along roadsides and fringes of forests nationwide.

Food uses: Fresh, cooked, or dried fruit eaten. Also squeezed into cider and commercially produced as juice. Eating whole apples may lower cholesterol due to their high soluble-fiber content.

Medicinal uses: Parts used are the fruit, dried peels, flowers, and leaves. Dried peels used in teas. Apple leaf tea has a mild binding effect. Finely ground fruit and commercially prepared apple pectin used to treat diarrhea, stomach and bowel gas, and digestive complaints. Slice whole apples, peel and all, and dry in a food dryer. Eat several slices after an oily dinner to improve digestion and sequester cholesterol. This treat is very soothing to stomach distress and has a slight binding effect.

AUTUMN OLIVE
Elaeagnaceae (*Elaeagnus umbellata*)

Identification: Bush or shrub to 18' tall. Long, ovate leaves, toothless and leathery, width less than half the length, length usually between ¾" and 1½"; leaves silvery underneath. Leaves, twigs, and berries are speckled; yellow-white flowers cluster in leaf axils. Scarlet speckled berries about the size of a currant ripen in September.

Habitat: Edges of woods and fencerows, in meadows, throughout the eastern United States and southern Canada, and roadsides to the Missouri River.

Food uses: Eat out of hand. Simmer berries to juice, strain away seeds with a food mill or sieve. Reduce sauce; use over pancakes, waffles, wontons, and egg rolls. Jam recipe: 8 cups berries mixed with ½ cup agar flakes. Bring to a boil in a pan, stirring continuously. Lower heat, cover, and simmer for 15 minutes, stirring occasionally. Strain seeds and use as a freezer jam.

Medicinal use: Antiscorbutic (Vitamin C content prevents scurvy.)

BEARBERRY, UVA URSI, KINNIKINNICK

Ericaceae (*Arctostaphylos uva-ursi*)

Identification: The plant is a trailing shrub, prostrate and mat forming. Leaves are dark, evergreen, leathery, smooth edged, obovate or spatula shaped, less than ¾" wide. Alpine variety of bearberry has larger leaves.

Habitat: I've found this plant in Michigan, Ontario, Oregon, Washington, and British Columbia and throughout the western and eastern mountain states.

Food uses: Leaves dried and mixed with tobacco for ritual Native American smoke. Berry is dry, mealy; was cooked with goose fat and other animal fats and eaten. Because of the berry's lack of flavor, mix with fish eggs and stronger-tasting foods to extend the nutrition. Dry berries in a food dryer and smash into flour-like substance. First People in the Northwest would use this flower like a spice on meat, liver. Leaves traditionally used in tea as a diuretic treatment for dropsy. Bella Coola tribe mixed berries in fat and ate them. Berries and leaves as a tea: tonic, diuretic, analgesic. Lower Chinook tribe dried berries then mixed them with fat for food. Native Americans boiled the berries with roots and vegetables to make a soup. First People ate the berries with fish eggs, preferably salmon eggs. Berries are sautéed in grease until crisp, then placed in cheesecloth (pantyhose will work) and pounded to break up berries. Add raw or cooked fish eggs and stir; pound to mix some more. Sweeten to taste.

Medicinal uses: Whole plant infused in water, then mixed with grease from a goose, duck, bear, or mountain goat and eaten. Infusion of aerial parts was gargled as mouthwash to treat canker sores and sore gums. Dried leaves and stems were ground and used as a poultice over wounds. Infusion of leaves, berries, and stems taken orally for cleaning kidneys and bladder complaints as a diuretic. Raw berries may be a laxative according to the Upper Tanana tribe. Raw leaves were chewed as a sialagogue to quench thirst when traveling. The infusion of the whole plant also taken to strengthen bones and bone breaks. Leaves and tobacco mixed and placed in all religious bundles for spiritual healing. Ritual smoking: leaves dried, toasted or roasted, crushed and smoked alone or mixed with tobacco. Pioneers considered the leaf infusion best known as diuretic, astringent, and tonic.

> ***Warning: Do not use during pregnancy and while nursing. Avoid acidic foods when using the tea to treat urogenital and biliary tract diseases. Prolonged use may damage liver and inflame and irritate bladder and kidneys. Not recommended for children.***

BLACKBERRY

Rosaceae (*Rubus allegheniensis, R. laciniatus*)

Identification: Similar to raspberry. Shrub with spiny branches; compound leaves, 5+/– leaflets, toothed (whereas raspberry typically has 3 leaves), and the white flower bloom appears after raspberries. *R. laciniatus* has sharply cut leaves. Blackberries found near your raspberry source. There are several species that ripen in mid- and late summer.

Habitat: Throughout the United States, fields, gardens, roadsides (more like side roads) fencerows, edges of woods.

Food uses: A low-calorie, high-nutrition breakfast made with blackberries. Mix 2 cups berries with 2 cups low-fat sweetened vanilla yogurt. Add a dash of milk and blend—a wonderful ice-cream substitute with half the sugar and fat. Also use in pies, muffins, pancakes, jellies, and jams. Make tea from the leaves.

Medicinal uses: Native Americans used roots with other herbs for eye sores, backaches, and stomachaches. Pioneers made blackberry vinegar to treat gout and arthritis. The Chinese use *Rubus* species in a tea to stimulate circulation—they claim it helps alleviate pain in muscles and bones. Blackberries also contain several cancer-fighting antioxidants.

BLUEBERRY

Ericaceae (*Vaccinium myrtillus, Vaccinium* spp.)

Identification: Deciduous small shrub with sharp-edged green branches. Leaves alternate, simple smooth margin; flowers white to pink, tightly clustered. Flowers are about ¼" long, greenish, tinged with pale pink, containing 8–10 stamens, shorter than the styles. Globular fruit is blue-black, often frosted, with numerous tiny seeds dispersed through the purple pulp.

Habitat: Northern tier of states from coast to coast. Find them in Acadia National Park on the East Coast and as far west as Vancouver Island. Found in wetlands, lowlands, highlands including eastern and western mountains. Wild or cultivated found in every state of the union.

Food uses: Fruit eaten fresh or dried. Leaves made into tea. Freeze or dry for storage; keep dried berries in freezer. Stir frozen berries into desserts for an ice cream–like chill and texture. Use to make pies, muffins, pancakes, and waffles.

Fold sour cream and blueberries into an omelet. Fruit antioxidant and a capillary protectant that may improve blood flow to distal areas (feet, brain, hands, etc.).

Medicinal uses: Native Americans used a decoction of fresh or dried berries to treat diarrhea. Iroquois used whole aerial part decoction as a topical application to dermatitis. Source of vitamin C. Dried pulverized leaves infused and taken for nausea. Folk use to prevent scurvy. Pioneers used leaves in decoction for treating diabetes. Berry tea used to treat mouth sores and inflammations.

CARRION FLOWER, SMOOTH CARRION FLOWER

Smilacaceae (*Smilax herbacea*)

Identification: This is a climbing vine (to 8') or tangled bush without thorns. Flowers (May–June) are born in round clusters and have a distinctive rotten odor.

Habitat: Grows in low, moist areas, margins of woods, roadsides, edges of wetlands, and meadows from Mason-Dixon Line north to Ontario, from the East Coast to the plains. Prefers rich, sandy loam. Pictured plant found 10 meters from lakeshore in northeast Indiana.

Note: Plant will come up in same location year after year.

Food uses: Berries are edible and remain on the plant throughout winter (although the longer you wait, the pulpier they get). Young shoots and leaves, like many others of the *Smilax* genus, are edible raw and unremarkable. Tuber is roasted, dried, and ground into flour—add to flour for pancakes, muffins, bread, waffles, and the like. While cross-country skiing through Michigan forests, *S. herbacea* is obvious against the white background, providing a pleasant trailside snack.

Medicinal uses: The *Smilax* genus has a long history of medicinal uses. Root decoction taken as an analgesic for backache. Crushed leaves rubbed over abrasions as an analgesic. Native Americans used parched and powdered leaves on inflammations and burns. Infusion of plant used to treat stomachache. Wilted leaves placed over boils. For further reference, see Daniel Moerman, *Native American Ethnobotany*.

WILD CHERRIES: BLACK CHERRY, CHOKECHERRY

Rosaceae (*Prunus serotina, P. virginiana*)

Identification: Bark of black cherry is rough, scaling. Peel the bark and the wood looks reddish underneath. Leaves ovate to lance shaped, toothed, smooth on top; midrib vein underneath has hairs. Leaf is also paler underneath. Berries are black, whereas chokecherries are reddish. Both berries hang from long, drooping racemes. Chokecherry is a smaller tree or shrub (black cherry may reach over 80'). Leaves are more oval, sharp toothed, sharper teeth than black cherry leaf, with no hairs on midrib. White flowers on thicker raceme. Bark of black cherry when freshly torn is aromatic, whereas chokecherry is not.

Chokecherry

Habitat: Cherry trees are typically a first-growth tree in the East replaced by maple and beech. They are widespread in woods, even open places. Choke-cherry found along streamsides in western dry areas—abundant along the Columbia River in Washington and the Clearwater River in Idaho.

Chokecherry leaf

Food uses: Bark, root, leaves inedible because of toxic glycoside prunasin, a hydrocyanic acid. Fruits of both plants are edible. Both make excellent jams, preserves. Put pitted cherries on cereal.

> *Warning: Do not eat seeds. Fruit may be dried and frozen for later use as a trail food. Use only pharmaceutical grade, professionally prepared formulations of this tree.*

Medicinal uses: Native Americans and pioneers used bark infusion as external wash. Black cherry: Inner bark used as a

Black cherry

flavoring and therapeutic for colds, sore throats, diarrhea, respiratory infections and congestion, as well as inflammations internally and externally.

CRANBERRY

Ericaceae (*Vaccinium oxycoccus*)

Identification: *Vaccinium oxycoccus,* an evergreen, dwarf shrub, creeps through bogs on slender stems, occasionally rising 5"–15". Bark is hairy to smooth and brown to black in color. Pink flowers are nodding, with petals sharply bent backward like shooting stars. Flowers are either solitary or in couplets, rarely 3. Fruit color ranges from pink to red, depending on ripeness. Small berries are juicy and very tart.

Habitat: Hidden along the floor of sphagnum bogs, hummocks at low elevations (up to 6,000' or 7,000'), including wet alpine meadows. They are widespread in acid bog habitats in the upper tier of states from coast to coast.

Food uses: Try it in your favorite apple crisp recipe, add black walnuts, and invite me over. Cranberries also spark up persimmon pudding. Dried cranberries good on pizzas, egg dishes, omelets, pancakes, oatmeal, waffles.

Medicinal uses: Berries and berry juice used as therapy for urinary tract infections—reported to acidify urine. Unverified claims suggest it helps remove kidney stones. Juice used to treat bladder infections and to prevent recurrence of urinary stones. It is antiscorbutic (has vitamin C to prevent or counteract scurvy). A study showed drinking the juice may prevent adhesion of *Escherichia coli* to gut lining and bladder lining. For detailed medicinal uses, see *Medicinal Plants of North America,* FalconGuides, by the author.

CURRANT

Grossulariaceae (*Ribes* spp.)

Identification: A member of the large gooseberry family, with more than 30 species. Leaves are alternate and lobed 3–7 times with palmate veins. Flowers are small, solitary, in clusters and variable in color and have 5 petals smaller than sepals. Fruits are round, waxy, seeded, smooth or spined, either red, yellow, black, or purple. Gooseberries have spined berries, and currants are smooth. All are shrubs from spreading to 10' tall.

Habitat: From valley floor to 6,000', various species are found; typically the best locations are near streams and rivers, rockslides, burnouts, stream banks, forests nationwide.

Food uses: Many currants are poor tasting—if the plant and fruit smells bad, it probably tastes the same. Eat out of hand, on breakfast cereals, in pancakes and waffles; the better-tasting fruits dried or frozen for later use.

Medicinal uses: A nontoxic fruit used as a panacea by Native Americans. The fruit contains ample amounts of gamma linolenic acid (GLA), useful in treating a variety of illnesses including diabetes, arthritis, alcoholism, eczema, and PMS.

ELDER, BLACK

Caprifoliaceae (*Sambucus canadensis*)

Identification: *Sambucus nigra* (introduced European variety and most studied) and *S. canadensis* are similar. Shrub or small tree to 25' in height; bark light brown to gray, fissured, and flaky. Branches break easily and die every autumn; when young they are green with gray lenticels. Leaves are matte green above and light blue green underneath. Leaves are oblong, ovate, and serrated. White flowers and fruit are in large rounded clusters. Fruit is oval, black to deep violet.

Habitat: *S. canadensis* typically found in wet thickets, along edges of streams, rivers, and lakes. Numerous other species found coast to coast, typically in wet areas, along creeks, rivers, in lowlands, and mountains of the West.

Food uses: Use elder flowers and berries sparingly as food because safety is not universally established—eat at your own risk. I eat the white cluster of blossoms dipped in tempura batter (thin coating) then frittered. Sprinkle and serve as a health-protecting, heart-stimulating dessert. Cook berries then strain juice through a sieve; thicken with pectin to combine with jams and marmalades. Cooked juice also added to maple

syrup. Juice, brown sugar, ginger, mustard, and soy combination provides a good wonton dip.

> *Warning: Leaves and stems toxic—cyanide poisoning. Cook berries before consumption. The western variety with red berries may be more toxic than blue and black berries—avoid eating red elderberries.*

Medicinal uses: Flowers reported to lower fever and reduce inflammation and are alterative and diuretic when infused into tea. Tea for influenza, colds, excess mucus, arthritis, asthma, bronchitis, improved heart function, fevers, hay fever, allergies, and sinusitis. Flowers infused in water and rubbed on skin soothe and soften irritations. Native Americans scraped bark and used root in infusion as emetic and laxative. Berry infusion used to treat rheumatism. Flower infusion induced sweats and used on colicky babies. Root pounded, decocted, and applied to swollen breasts, and leaves in infusion as a wash for sores.

GOOSEBERRY, PRICKLY

Grossulariaceae (*Ribes cynosbati*)

Identification: Shrub; spiny branches; spiny fruit, round to the size of a nickel in diameter, while its close relative, currant, has smooth or spined fruit; deeply lobed leaves, sharply toothed; flowers yellow, purplish, or white (depending on species). You can find gooseberries and currants in woodlands and along the margins of woods. There are numerous species. The spiny, dangerous-looking berries are harmless and ready for harvest in early summer.

Habitat: Various species found throughout the United States in woodlands, along stream edges, and bordering wetlands.

Food uses: Make gooseberry-currant pie. Be certain to add lemon juice to punch up the taste. When fully ripe eat out of hand, made into jams and jelly, and as a marinade ingredient for wild game and cuts of meat.

Medicinal uses: Gooseberries and currants are made into a jelly spiced with peppermint, lemon juice, and ginger, then taken as a sore throat remedy. Others claim that gamma linolenic acid (GLA), an active ingredient of currants, may prevent acne, obesity, and schizophrenia.

GRAPE, WILD
Vitaceae (*Vitis* spp.)

Identification: Climbing vine; clinging tendrils; green flowers in a large cluster; leaves alternate, simple, round, toothed, with heart-shaped base. The young leaves and ripe fruits are edible. Vines found clinging to and climbing trees, walls, and fences.

Warning: The Canadian moonseed plant looks like wild grape but is poisonous. Learn to distinguish these 2 plants before eating what you think are wild grapes. Squash the moonseed fruit and look at the seed—see the crescent moon—beware. Get expert identification.

Habitat: Hardwood forest fringes and interior in eastern United States, roughly to Missouri.

Food uses: To make raisins, cover wild grapes with cheesecloth and dry them in the sun for 3 days, or dry them in a food dryer. Grape leaves wrapped around rice, vegetables, and meat and steamed until tender. Add grape leaves to pickling spices when preparing dill pickles.

Medicinal uses: Fruit, leaves, and tendrils used by Native Americans and pioneers to treat hepatitis, diarrhea, and snakebites. Native Americans used tonic made with grape and several other herbs to increase fertility. Tannins and other phenolic compounds found in grape skins may provide protection from heart disease. Resveratrol from grapes may prevent strokes and heart attacks.

GROUND CHERRY, CHINESE LANTERN PLANT
Solanaceae (*Physalis* spp.)

Identification: A member of the tomato family and close relative of the tomatillo, the ground cherry is similar to a tomato plant but stiffer and more erect. It is either an annual or perennial and has fuzzy leaves and bears a small tomato-like fruit enclosed in a papery husk that develops from the calyx.

Habitat: Prefers full sun; found along edges of gardens and vacant lots; species is tolerant of both cold and heat. Plant grows in poor and depleted soils, waste ground.

Food uses: Fruit is edible; mild flavor, with a hint of strawberry. Amish friends make them into pies with copious amounts of sugar (extra lemon juice necessary). Also eaten raw and in salads. Slice onto pizzas, add to sauces, chop into stews, and mix raw into mixed-fruit dishes. Use as a substitute for tomatillos in green salsa.

Medicinal uses: As a poultice over abscesses, a tea for coughs, and a drink for fevers and sore throats. Native Americans (Omaha) used *P. lanceolata* root decoction to treat headaches and stomachaches.

HAWTHORN
Rosaceae (*Crataegus laevigata;* more than 1,000 species)

Identification: Shrubs to small trees, 6'–20'; many branched, branches thorned; 3–5-lobed leaves with forward pointing lobes, serrated leaf edges; leaves are yellow-green and glossy. White flowers are numerous, in terminal clusters, with 10–20 stamens, and give rise to small apple-like fruit. Fruit is ovoid to round, red or black, and mealy. There is 1 seed in each chamber of the ovary.

Habitat: *Crataegus macrosperma* typically found east of the Mississippi in damp woods and fringes of forests across the western states. Other varieties found nationwide.

Food uses: Eaten out of hand, mealy and seedy, but heart-protecting value makes it worth the culinary failure. Fruit sliced and dried and decocted or infused in water to make a health-protecting drink, use with green tea; berry has a sour to sweet flavor, and several varieties are bland. Herb in Europe and China, hawthorn has long been used to treat heart disease. The active phytochemicals are bioflavonoids.

> *Warning: Extract may be a uterine stimulant, may induce menstruation, contraindicated for pregnant women.*

HIGH BUSH CRANBERRY
Caprifoliaceae (*Viburnum trilobum*)

Identification: Shrub with obvious 3-lobed, coarse, and toothed leaves (2"–4" long). Leaf lobes pointed. White flowers in flat clusters. Fruit turns red and is best after a frost or 2.

Habitat: Lakesides, roadsides, edges of marshes and thickets, lakeshores. Stands of these shrubs grow in profusion and large, with huge tart berries along the coast of Lake Superior in the Pictured Rocks National Lakeshore (find them near the lighthouse).

Food uses: This is a Thanksgiving fruit, and I feel certain it was part of that first historic meal. The tart berries, best after a frost, go great in stuffing and marinades. They're made into jellies and infused into cold drinks. Remove seeds and simmer berries for best results—add sugar and lime juice, and reduce to a surprisingly fresh, tart, and delicious sauce.

Medicinal uses: Fruit is high in vitamin C. The plant is an escaped European gone wild. Fruit used in decoction to lower fevers. Bark decoction is a laxative and used to treat stomach cramps.

HUCKLEBERRY, EVERGREEN HUCKLEBERRY

Ericaceae (*Vaccinium ovatum*)

Identification: Bushy evergreen shrub to 7'. Twigs hairy, reddish in color; leaves evergreen, finely toothed, ½"–1" long, oval, thick, waxy; bell-shaped pink flowers. Blooms May–July depending on altitude and weather. Small, sweet, shiny black berries. Favorite bear food.

Habitat: Typically West Coast and mountain states from Alaska to California.

Food uses: Eat out of hand or in hot and cold cereals, or use to make jam. Marinade recipe: Simmer 1 cup berries; stir in 1 teaspoon Dijon mustard, 1 tablespoon soy sauce, 1 tablespoon crushed ginger, and the juice of half a lemon. Use marinade on salmon and chicken or as dip for wontons.

Medicinal uses: High in antioxidants, including anthocyanin. For diabetics these berries may help manage blood-sugar levels.

JUNEBERRY, SERVICEBERRY

Rosaceae (*Amelanchier* spp.)

Identification: Produces prodigious crops of fruit across North America. Various species are trees or shrubs. They have showy flowers, white to cream colored, drooping with 5 lance-shaped petals. Leaves are oval, alternate, toothed—prominently at end of leaf—and entire or smooth toward the base. Fruit black to dark purple, 2 seeded, and juicy. Early April flowers in the Midwest and later in the Mountain West. Fruits available all summer depending on longitude and latitude.

Habitat: The plant prefers moist soil or rocky areas, fringes of wooded areas and near water sources, from sea level to alpine elevations. *Amelanchier alnifolia* grows in profusion along the Columbia River in Washington and along the Clearwater and Selway Rivers in Idaho. At Hyalite Reservoir, the South Shore Trail shares the fruit with you.

Food uses: Berry is edible and a welcome addition to pancakes, waffles, muffins, and game dishes (venison or buffalo). Try them with breakfast cereal. Cook berries down with honey or maple syrup to make preserves; add lemon or lime juice. Mix with huckleberries and other fruit for field berry pie. Cambium of shrub considered nutritious and given to Native American babies. For further reference, see Daniel Moerman's *Native American Ethnobotany,* p. 67.

Medicinal uses: Native Americans boiled berries and used decoction as an antiseptic, typically for earaches and colds. Teething babies sipped on a decoction of the roots. Sharpened twigs used to puncture pustules on people and animals. Boiled bark taken for stomachaches.

JUNIPER

Cupressaceae (*Juniper communis*)

Identification: An evergreen tree or low-lying, spreading shrub, often in colonies. It has flat needles in whorls of 3, spreading from the branches. Leaves are evergreen, pointy, stiff, somewhat flattened and light green; some say sea green. Buds are covered with scalelike needles. Berries are blue, hard, and when scraped with a fingernail they emit a tangy smell and impart a tangy flavor—a somewhat creosote-like taste. Male flowers are catkin-like with numerous stamens in 3 segmented whorls. Female flowers are green and oval.

Habitat: Found across the United States. Often found in dune blowouts along the shore of Lake Michigan and throughout eastern and western mountains. It easily relocates to gardens and yards.

Food uses: Dried berries cooked with game and fowl. Try putting them in a pepper mill and grating them into bean soup, stews, on wild game and domestic fowl. To make berries into tea, simply crush 2 berries and add to hot water or to green tea just off the boil. Juniper berries infused into vodka to flavor it. Gin, schnapps, and Aquavit also flavored with juniper berries. Berries also used in grilling marinades.

When grated it is added to cold cuts. Try it as a spice on vegetated protein cold cuts, like Wham and mock chicken, garden burgers. Large amounts of the berry may be toxic—use in small amounts like a spice.

Medicinal uses: Native Americans used juniper branches around tepees and shelters to fend off rattlesnakes. The diluted essential oil applied to skin to draw and cleanse deeper skin tissue. It used to promote menstruation to relieve premenstrual syndrome and dysmenorrhea. Traditional practitioners use 1 teaspoon of berries to 1 cup of water, boil for 3 minutes, let steep until cool. Some practitioners add bark and needles to berry tea. The berry is antiseptic, diuretic, a tonic and digestive aid—strongly antiseptic to urinary tract problems and gallbladder complaints, but contraindicated for kidney disease.

> *Warning: Avoid during pregnancy. The herb may induce contractions and may increase menstrual bleeding. Do not use if kidney infection or kidney disease is suspected. Do not use the concentrated and caustic essential oil internally.*

MAYAPPLE
Berberidaceae (*Podophyllum peltatum*)

Identification: Large pair of dissected, parasol-like leaves; white flower on petiole between leaves; yellow-green fruit. Mayapple parts are, for the most part, poisonous. The 2 large, parasol-like leaves shelter a white flower that bears an edible fruit when ripe in midsummer. Pick the fruit when soft and ripe.

Habitat: Forest-dwelling plant, found in most states, except extreme desert, southern California, and lower Florida.

Food uses: Expert foragers carefully gather ripe fruit for use in pie fillings and jellies. Fruit ripe in late June or July, but hurry, as every raccoon and their friends are competing with you.

> *Warning: Except for the pulp of the ripe fruit, this plant is poisonous.*

Medicinal uses: An analog of etoposide, the active agent of mayapple, is used to treat testicular and small lung cancer.

MOUNTAIN ASH
Rosaceae (*Sorbus sitchensis, S. americana, S. decora*)

Identification: Shrub or small tree to 40'. Compound leaves, 11–17 toothed leaflets; leaves long and narrow, 3 times longer than broad; flowers and fruit in rounded clusters. Berries are red when ripe, best after a frost.

Habitat: *S. sitchensis* is found in the western United States, at higher elevations and moist areas. *S. americana* found in northern tier of the eastern states, typically around moist areas; abundant along the coast of Lake Superior.

Food uses: Berries are best after a frost (or you can freeze in the freezer and thaw them). Their high pectin content makes them a good addition to preserves and jellies. Mix about ¼ cup mountain ash berries to 1 cup blueberries or cherries. Boiled berries used as relish for meat, sweeten to taste; very good over goose and duck. Green or ripe fruit may be mashed and used to marinate meat.

Medicinal uses: Native Americans used the inner bark and gummy terminal buds of *S. americana* as a tonic. The tonic is reported to enhance mood and treat depression. Bark and bud infusion is considered antimicrobial and an appetite stimulant. Inner bark and/or gummy red terminal buds infused for colds. Inner bark infusion used to reduce pain after childbirth; root infusion used to treat colic. Root and bark decoction used for treating rheumatism and arthritis. Wood ash is styptic and considered useful for treating burns and boils. Root of sweet flag and *S. americana* were combined and infused as spring tonic. Berries used as a digestive aid. Twigs of western species used as chewing stick (toothbrush).

OREGON GRAPE
Berberidaceae (*Mahonia aquifolium, M. nervosa* var. *nervosa*)

Identification: To 6' tall (*Mahonia aquifolium*) evergreen shrub, with holly-like, shiny leaves; leaves leathery, pinnate, compound, pointed edges. Flower is small, bright yellow. Berries deep blue, waxy. Gray stem. Roots and root hairs, when peeled, are bright yellow inside due to alkaloid berberine. *M. nervosa* is a smaller forest dweller with a rosette of compound leaves in a whorl up to 3' tall; berries on central spikes.

Habitat: *M. nervosa* found in open forests and graveyards, with numerous sites found along Mount Baker Highway in Washington en route to Mount Baker. *M. aquifolium* is found along roadsides, forest edges from Washington State into Idaho and Montana.

Food uses: Tart berries of *M. aquifolium* eaten in late summer. Native Americans smashed the berries and dried them for later use. They may be boiled with ample amounts of sugar into jam (or honey); the juice is tart. Carrier Indians of the Northwest simmered young leaves and ate them. The smaller creeping *M. nervosa* prepared and eaten in the same way and is preferred but not as abundant. Try berries mixed with other fruit to improve taste. Berries are pounded to paste, formed into cakes, and dried for winter food.

Medicinal uses: When eaten raw in small amounts, the fruit is slightly emetic. Tart berries of both species considered a morning-after pick-me-up. Native Americans believed berries slightly emetic. A decoction of stem used as an antiemetic. These 2 bitter and astringent herbs are used in decoction to treat liver and gallbladder complaints. The bark infusion was used by Native Americans as an eyewash. According to traditional use, the decocted drug from the inner bark (berberine) stimulates the liver and gallbladder, cleansing them, releasing toxins, and increasing the flow of bile. *M. aquifolium* extractions are available in commercial ointments to treat dry skin, unspecified rashes, and psoriasis. Do not use during pregnancy. The bitter drug may prove an appetite stimulant, but little research has been done. Other unproven uses in homeopathic doses include the treatment of liver and gallbladder problems.

Notes: The shredded bark and roots of both species can also be simmered in water to make a bright-yellow dye.

PAWPAW

Annonaceae (*Asimina triloba*)

Identification: Small tree (10'–25') growing on riverbanks, along streams; as a secondary growth under taller trees, loves shade, does not tolerate sunlight. Leaves are alternate, simple, large (up to 12"), narrow at base and broad near tip. Flowers are elegant, large, and come early; worth the trip into the woods.

Habitat: Eastern and southern United States; understory in hardwood

forest, with numerous stands along the southeastern shore of Lake Michigan, just beyond the fringing dunes.

Food uses: Large fruit eaten raw, or remove seeds and cook like pudding, and then blend with yogurt. Pawpaw shakes blended with other berries are delicious and nutritious. Fruits frozen for future use. Let unripe fruits ripen in vegetable drawer of a refrigerator; once ripe, however, they spoil quickly.

Medicinal use: An anticancer substance has been isolated from pawpaw that is more than 1,000 times as potent as the synthetic drug Adriamycin.

PERSIMMON
Ebenaceae (*Diospyros virginiana*)

Identification: A small to medium (to 60') irregularly shaped tree with gray or black bark arranged in a blocky (mosaic) pattern with orange in the valleys between the blocks. Lateral branches are typically much smaller in diameter than the trunk. Flowers are 4 lobed and yellow. Leaves are stiff, oval, alternate and un-serrated. Fruit is orange, pulpy, and retains the flower's calyx, soft and darkens when ripe—astringent when unripe, sweet when ripe.

Habitat: Edges of woods, cultivated arboretums; tolerates dryness, prefers well-drained soil. Persimmon trees found as far north as the protected temperate areas of the Great Lakes. Lower Michigan is the upper limit of this tree's range.

Food uses: Leaves make a refreshing tea. Native Americans fermented this fruit in water to make an alcoholic drink—roll fruit in cornmeal and soak in water to ferment. Fruit is edible late in the season when the cold takes the "pucker" off its taste. Pudding made from the fruit is delicious. Collect fruit after a frost when it is soft and sweet. Best picked off the ground, then you know it is ready.

Medicinal uses: Syrup made from unripe fruit said to be therapeutic treatment of diarrhea. Astringency of the fruit may explain this use. Infusion of the bark used to treat liver problems (folk and Native American tradition). Astringency of fruit made for a sore throat gargle after infusing mashed fruit in water. Bark chewed for gastro-intestinal stress, acid reflux of the stomach.

RASPBERRY
Rosaceae (*Rubus idaeus, R. occidentalis*)

Identification: Shrub with spiny branches; compound leaves, 3–5 leaflets, sharply toothed; white flowers, 3 or more petals. Berry pulls free from stem and has a hollow center.

Habitat: Red and black raspberries found along the fringes of woods, fencerows, and the margins of fields. Berries are ready for harvest in late spring and early summer throughout the United States.

Food uses: Use as pie filling, or stir into pancake batter and muffin mixes. Makes excellent jam or jelly.

Medicinal uses: Leaves are steeped in tea and used as a tonic for pregnant women. Native Americans used root for diarrhea and dysentery. Also used to flavor medicines. Like other berries, it's a great dietary choice for weight watchers—it's high in cancer-fighting ellagic acid. One cup of raspberries per day shows promise as an anticancer agent. Nananone, the frosty appearance of wild raspberries, is an anti-fungal agent that protects the berries from fungal infections. That's why wild raspberries do not spoil as quickly as cultivars that have lost their capacity to produce nananone.

ROSE, WILD ROSE, WRINKLED ROSE, DOG ROSE
Rosaceae (*Rosa* spp., *Rosa rugosa*)

Identification: A sprawling or climbing shrub with thorns, conspicuous flowers, and famous for the rose hip, its fruiting body. Leaves are ovate, finely serrated.

Habitat: Widespread and numerous species from coast to coast.

Food uses: Flower petals are edible, as is the fruiting body. Flower petals candied: Mix high-proof grain alcohol with sugar until hypertonic solution (sugar no longer dissolves in solution).

Paint rose with sugar-alcohol solution and let dry. Extract rose water from rose petals with an inexpensive over-the-counter still. See our DVD *Cooking with Edible Flowers* for details (it's listed in Appendix C: References and Resources). Rosewater flavors desserts, piecrusts, chicken dishes.

Medicinal uses: Rosewater used as a wash to protect the skin; fruits eaten as a source of vitamin C and to stem diarrhea; bark tea drunk for dysentery. A decoction of bark imbibed to treat worms; root tea as eyewash. Floral tea used by this author as stimulant and tonic: It may promote improved circulation, reduce rheumatic pain, stem dysentery, and relieve stomachache. Petal infusion may relieve inflammation of the mouth and pharynx.

SALAL
Ericaceae (*Gaultheria shallon*)
Identification: Sprawling shrub forms dense thickets in northwestern pine forests. Oval, shiny, leathery, thick leaves are alternate, clinging to sturdy stems on petioles of varying lengths. Bell-shaped pink to white flowers strung out like pearls near ends of stem. Dark-blue to blue-black fruit is ripe from July through September.

Habitat: Seashore west of the Cascades and coastal ranges; under Douglas fir and cedar from California to the Alaskan peninsula.

Food uses: The berries eaten as you hike along. Take some home and blend them into jelly or maple syrup, or dry them in a food dryer and use them in muffins, waffles, or pancakes. Another tasty addition to marinades; berries also used to make wine.

Medicinal uses: Native Americans chewed the leaves to stem off hunger. Dried salal berries are considered a good laxative, while the plant's dried leaves infused in water can be imbibed to treat diarrhea (the tea is astringent, thus its effectiveness). Dried leaves powdered and used externally as a styptic on scrapes and abrasions. Also, dried leaf powder mixed with water to make a pasty poultice for wounds.

SALMONBERRY

Rosaceae (*Rubus spectabilis*)
Identification: Shrub 6'–7' in height, found along moist slopes, sunny banks, and streams. Brown stems with yellow bark, laced with weak-to-soft thorns; leaflets fuzzy with serrated edges, usually in threes, approximately 3" in length. Fuchsia flowers arrive with leaves in spring. Soft, dry fruit ranges from bright red to yellowish. ***Note:*** I find this berry on Vancouver Island along the path to Botanical Beach. To find the berries, look for bear dung.

Habitat: Moist edges of woods, seeps, edges of meadows, streamsides from Michigan west to the Sierras and Rockies north to Alaska.

Food uses: The soft (when ripe) fruit melts in your mouth and will melt in your backpack too—best eaten as you hike along. Spring sprouts peeled, cooked, and eaten. Harvest the stems before they become hard and woody, and eat them raw, steamed, or roasted.

Medicinal uses: Root bark decoction taken for stomach ailments. Poultice of bark applied to toothache. For further reference, see Daniel Moerman's *Native American Ethnobotany.*

SPICEBUSH

Lauraceae (*Lindera benzoin*)
Identification: Shrub found in rich woodlands and along streams. Grows to 15', with numerous spreading branches. Smooth branches give off spicy odor when soft bark is scratched with thumbnail. Leaves smooth, bright green, pointed (widest near or above middle section), simple, alternate, deciduous, 2½"–5 ½" long and 1½"–

2½" wide. Flowers small, yellow, in dense clusters along previous year's twigs. Fruits in clusters, widest in middle (somewhat football shaped but with more rounded ends); start out green and become bright red in autumn. Flowers appear in early spring, before leaves.

Habitat: Eastern United States, roughly to the Mississippi River. In rich, moist forest as understory in birch, beech, and hardwood forest.

Food uses: In the spring gather end twigs, tie them together with string, and throw them in a pot with leeks, nettles, mushrooms, and dandelions. Bundles of stems can be steeped in boiling water to make tea (sweeten with honey). Young leaves can be used in the same way. In the fall try drying the fruits in a food dryer. Dry fruits are hard and can be ground in a coffee mill and used as a substitute for allspice. Fruits also used in meat marinades. Try it with your ribs recipe—like juniper berries, 3–5 berries is sufficient. Chew green end twigs as a chew stick while you walk to freshen your mouth and cleanse your teeth.

Medicinal uses: Native Americans used the bark in infusion for treating colds, coughs, and dysentery. Tea made from the bark was used as a spring tonic. Bathing in this tea reportedly helps rheumatism. Tea made from the twigs was used to treat dysmenorrhea.

STAGHORN SUMAC
Anacardiaceae (*Rhus typhina*)
Identification: Shrub or small tree; leaves lance shaped, alternate, compound, numerous leaflets, toothed; cone-shaped flower and berry clusters. The large berry spikes of staghorn sumac are ready to harvest in late summer.

Habitat: Entire United States, except extreme desert, southern California, and lower Florida.

Food uses: Strip red staghorn sumac berries from heads. Discard stems and heads. Soak cotton-covered berries in hot water to extract a lemonade-like drink. Steep sassafras root in the tea. Add sugar and serve.

Medicinal uses: Staghorn sumac flower can be steeped into tea and taken for stomach pain. Gargles made from berries are purported to help sore throats.

STRAWBERRY
Rosaceae (*Fragaria virginiana, F. vesca, F. californica*)
Identification: White flower; sharply toothed leaflets in threes, growing in colonies; looks like the store-bought variety but smaller.

Habitat: *F. virginiana* found in the eastern United States, roughly to the Mississippi; *F. vesca* found west of the Mississippi River; and *F. californica* found in California and Baja. Look for strawberries in meadows and open woods. Harvest in late May and early June.

Food uses: Strawberries are high in vitamin C and are fiber rich—a good choice for dieters. A wet spring will bring a robust harvest. Use on cereals, with yogurt, on pancakes and waffles, in summer drinks, and with ice cream.

Medicinal uses: Native Americans used strawberries to treat gout, scurvy, and kidney infections. Root tannins were used to treat malaria. The fruits contain ellagic acid.

THIMBLEBERRY
Rosaceae (*Rubus parviflorus*)

Identification: Found in moist places (streamside, lakeside, and coastal)—a deciduous shrub up to 7' high, barbless stems, erect with shredded-to-smooth bark. Leaves are large, maple-like, smooth or slightly hairy on top, fuzzy underneath. Picked berry fits on your finger like a thimble.

Habitat: Mountain West, primarily the Sierras and Rockies to Alaska.

Food uses: Eat the soft, ripe berries in the bush. Like salmonberry (see above), thimbleberry will turn to mush in your backpack. To eat: Apply forefinger and thumb to fruit, pull and twist, and pop in your mouth. No cooking required. Try this tart berry on cereal. Northwestern Native Americans dried the berries in cakes or stored them in goose grease. Young shoots harvested, peeled, and cooked as a spring green.

Medicinal uses: Kwakiutl nation of the Northwest made a decoction, a boiled drink for treating bloody vomiting, that included blackberry roots, vines, and thimbleberry.

WINTERGREEN AND SPOTTED WINTERGREEN
Ericaceae (*Gaultheria procumbens, Chimaphila maculata*)

Identification: Evergreen; long oval leaves, finely serrated margins; drooping white flowers. The flower forms an edible berry that turns from white to red by late summer. Available all winter—if not gobbled up by late-season foragers.

Wintergreen

Habitat: Entire United States, except extreme desert, southern California, and lower Florida. There are several species of this plant in North America. Creeping wintergreen, or checkerberry, found in the eastern half of the United States.

Food uses: Add summer fruits to pancake and muffin mixes. Use the leaves to make a delicate tea, or munch them (don't swallow) as a breath freshener.

Medicinal uses: Astringent, counter-irritant. Never take oil internally. Tea from leaves used for flu and colds and as a stomach alkalizer. Analgesic and rubefacient oil for muscular pain and arthritic pain; also a flavoring agent for cough drops.

Spotted wintergreen

Wetlands

AMERICAN WHITE WATER LILY

Nymphaeaceae (*Nymphaea odorata*)

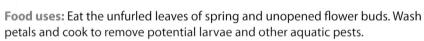

Identification: Large white flower to 5" in diameter with numerous petals and yellow reproductive parts; roots submerged in freshwater; leaves flat, platter shaped, 6"–10" across.

Habitat: Found floating on still or gently moving shallow water to 3' in depth. Found across the northern tier of states, farther south in the East, and rarely in the Southwest.

Food uses: Eat the unfurled leaves of spring and unopened flower buds. Wash petals and cook to remove potential larvae and other aquatic pests.

Medicinal uses: Dried and powdered root sucked in mouth to relieve mouth sores. Juice of root used to treat colds. Numerous tribes used the root juice, decoction, and powdered roots in many ways, primarily to treat colds and coughs.

ARROWHEAD, WAPATO, DUCK POTATOES

Alismataceae (*Sagittaria latifolia*)

Identification: Arrow-shaped leaves, widely and deeply cleft, veins palmate; white, platter-shaped flowers with 3 petals; deep-set tube growing up from a soft bottom.

Habitat: Edges of slow-moving streams, ponds, and along shorelines of lakes with soft bottom edges; ranges across northern tier of states, from Maine to Washington.

Food uses: Harvest tuber in fall or early spring. Boil until tender, pluck away skin, and sauté or smash and cook like hash browns. Native Americans roasted the tubers, peeled them, and ate out of hand.

Medicinal uses: Root said to settle the stomach, alleviate indigestion. Poultice of root applied to cuts and abrasions.

CATTAILS
Typhaceae (*Typha angustifolia, T. latifolia*)

Identification: Wetland grass with long sword-shaped leaves, 2-headed flower, male spike on top and female just below. Grows to 7'; flower heads develop in May and June, later in the mountain states.

Habitat: Numerous species worldwide. Broadleaf *(Typha angustifolia)* and narrow leaf *(T. latifolia)* are common across the central and northern-tier states. Found along streams, in marshes, fens, bogs, and other wetlands with still or slow-moving water.

Food uses: Collect the male flowering parts in late May and June in Michigan, about 2 or 3 pounds, and then freeze. Add the male parts to pizza dough, bread dough, cookies, and biscuits—anything you bake—to enrich the final product with essential amino acids and bioflavonoids. Strip young shoots (through June) of their tough outer leaves down to the delicate core. Eat on the spot or sauté or stir-fry. Roots are starch rich and provide needed energy for beavers, muskrats, and humans. The young (June) female flower spike is boiled and eaten like corn on the cob; alas it does not taste like corn on the cob, but once again, it may be the difference between starving and survival.

Male and female heads; **Typha latifolia** *(left) and* **Typha angustifolia** *(right)*

Medicinal uses: The mucilaginous chopped root applied to wounds, minor abrasions, inflammations, and burns. Burned cattail ash is styptic and used to stop bleeding and disinfect wounds.

Note: Dried cattail fluff is an excellent fire accelerator; use in the fire nest.

CHUFA SEDGE, YELLOW NUT SEDGE

Cyperaceae (*Cyperus esculentus*)

Identification: Green flower with numerous spikes. Grows to 3', with flat seeds surrounded by 4 bracts at 90 degrees to one another; leaves are slender, tough, grasslike (but not a grass), and grow from an underground tuber.

Habitat: In or near wetlands, escaped to gardens—prefers damp soil. Found coast to coast, in all states except perhaps Montana and Wyoming.

Food uses: Roots dried, ground, and cooked with other food; or simply dig roots, wash, and eat raw. They are also baked or boiled.

Medicinal uses: Pima and other tribes chewed roots to treat colds.

CINQUEFOIL

Rosaceae (*Potentilla canadensis, P. anserina*)

Identification: Leaves on long, jointed stolons (delicate stem-like appendages). Two types of leaves: oval or elliptical (which are much smaller and have sharply toothed leaflets up to 1¼" long), with small buttercup-like flower. Both species can be found on waste ground or in gravelly or sandy habitats.

Habitat: *Potentilla canadensis* found in the eastern United States to the Mississippi in fields, waste ground, roadsides, and meadows.

Food uses: *P. canadensis* is used to make a gold-colored tea that is high in calcium. For a quick roast, cook the leaves in a hot (covered) Dutch oven for 2–3 minutes or pour boiling water over the leaves. *P. anserina* roots are edible. Gather the roots, wash them thoroughly, and steam in a wok. Native Americans steamed the roots in cedar boxes and served them with duck fat. To this day the Ditidaht peoples of British Columbia gather and prepare the roots in this traditional way.

Medicinal uses: Roots are rich in tannins and are used by some naturopathic physicians to treat diarrhea, Crohn's disease, colitis, gastritis, and peptic ulcers. Use only under the supervision of a trained holistic health-care practitioner.

DUCKWEED

Lemnaceae (*Lemna trisulca*)

Identification: One of the smallest flowering plants, it covers still water and turns pond surfaces green by early summer—from a distance it looks like green pond scum. Up close it is a single or double leaf floating on the surface of the water, with 2 root hairs siphoning nutrients from the water. It is the habitat of many larval forms of life, so cooking is imperative. Size: smaller than the nail on your pinky, to 1 centimeter.

Habitat: Surface of still freshwater. Found coast to coast.

Food uses: Thoroughly wash, then cook in soups and stews. What I consider a survival food, and there is plenty of it. It's texture is crunchy, especially when larval snails are not removed from the food.

Medicinal uses: In poultice and applied to swellings and inflammations.

HORSETAIL, SCOURING RUSH, EQUISETUM

Equisetaceae (*Equisetum hyemale, E. arvense*)

Identification: The plant my brother and I called snakeweed when kids, the segmented stem can be pulled apart and put back together at the joints to make necklaces and bracelets. It appears in the spring as a naked segmented stem with a dry-tipped sporangium with spores. Later the sterile stage stems arise with many long needlelike branches arranged in whorls up the stem.

Habitat: Found around marshes, fens, bogs, streams, lakes, streams, rivers, and in my garden.

Food uses: Native Americans of the Northwest eat the tender young shoots of the plant as a blood purifier (tonic). The tips (the strobili) are boiled and eaten in Japan-mix vinegar and soy; boil

5 minutes and enjoy. Native Americans of the Southwest eat the roots.

Medicinal uses: Mexican Americans use dried whole aerial plant parts of horsetail in infusion or decoction to treat painful urination. Therapy not supported by scientific evidence. But equisetonin and bioflavonoids in the plant may account for its diuretic effect. Native Americans used a poultice of the stem to treat rashes of the armpit

and groin, and an infusion of the stem was used by Blackfoot as a diuretic. Cherokee used aerial part infusion to treat coughs in their horses. Infusion of the plant used to treat dropsy, backaches, cuts, and sores. Baths of the herb reported to treat syphilis and gonorrhea. This is one of the First People's most widely used herbs.

JEWELWEED, SPOTTED-TOUCH-ME-NOTS

Balsaminaceae (*Impatiens capensis*)

Identification: Fleshy annual of wetlands to 7' in height. Simple green, almost translucent stems with swollen nodes. Deep-green leaves are thin, ovate, with 5–14 teeth. Plants grow in dense colonies, often with stinging nettle. Flowers are orange-yellow with reddish-brown spots. They are spur shaped and irregular, with the spur curving back and lying parallel to the sac. Flower is about ½" wide and ¾" in length. Fruit is oblong capsule that when ripe bursts open and disperses the seeds.

Young jewelweed shoots

Habitat: Lowlands, wetlands, edges of lakes and streams, wet fens, edges of bogs, and relocates to the garden, providing food and medicine. Young shoots of spring bolt form a complete ground cover in wet lowlands, along streams, wetlands, lakes.

Jewelweed flower

Food uses: Eat the small flowers of summer in salads and stir-fry. Pick the young shoots of spring and add to your mushroom soup, egg dishes, stir-fry, or sauté with spring vegetables.

Medicinal uses: Traditional treatment for poison ivy. Crush and rub the aerial parts of plants over inflamed area of dermatitis for an immediate anti-inflammatory effect, reducing itching and inflammation. The Creek tribe used an infusion of smashed spicebush berries and jewelweed as a bath for congestive heart failure. Crushed flowers used on bruises, cuts, and burns. Repeated applications of the juice may remove warts. Whole herb infused as an appetite stimulant and diuretic. Used by naturopaths to treat dyspepsia.

LABRADOR TEA

Ericaceae (*Ledum groenlandicum, L. glandulosum*)

Identification: Evergreen shrub 15"–30" or more; flowers with 5 petals (⅜" wide) that form flat terminal clusters; fruits in round nodding capsules—leaves evergreen, oval to lance shaped down rolled edges, wooly underneath.

Habitat: Found in boggy areas of the western mountains and northern tier of eastern states and southern Canadian provinces.

Food uses: Leaves and flowers are used to make tea. Labrador tea is preferred over glandular Labrador tea, as it is slightly toxic and mildly narcotic, causing stomach distress and even death from an overdose. Be careful, as these species can be confused with bog laurels.

Medicinal uses: Native Americans used the leaf and floral tea to treat acute infections such as colds and sore throats. Smoking the dried leaves claimed to induce euphoria. Crushed and powdered leaves were used as snuff to treat inflammation of the nasal passages. Tea said to help alleviate allergies. The tea is diuretic, laxative, and a smooth muscle relaxant. According to Kershaw in *Edible and Medicinal Plants of the Rockies,* crushed leaves used by Scandinavians to flavor schnapps—the alcoholic nightcap is used as a sleep aid. Alcohol extracts used to treat numerous skin conditions including inflammation, scabies, fungus, chiggers, and lice bites. Powdered roots were applied to ulcers. And fresh leaves are chewed as a general tonic.

MARSH MARIGOLD

Ranunculaceae (*Caltha palustris*)

Identification: One of first plants to flower in the spring, it has broadly heart-shaped leaves ¾"–1½ " wide. Bright-yellow flowers to 1½" wide, sepals are petal-like; blooms in early spring. Many seeded fruits, in a recurved capsule forming in early summer.

Habitat: In marshes, swamps, along edges of all sorts of wetlands: stream banks, lakeshores. Found north to Alaska, from Washington State to the East Coast and as far south as the Carolinas.

Food uses: Early flowering buds are pickled. I use dill brine (reuse the juice in an empty pickle jar), boil the brine, add dried buds (dry in a food dryer) for 3 minutes at boil, pour juice and rehydrated buds back into pickle jar, and refrigerate. Native Americans cooked leaves and also ate seeds. Leaves cooked in animal fats. On the other hand, a few tribes considered the plant too toxic to eat (see warning).

> *Warning: All parts of this plant are toxic (with protoanemonin and helleborine). When the bud is dried, the volatile toxic principles denature or gas off, making buds edible. The 3 minutes in brine is an extra measure I take. After all that work, mix a martini, drop in a bud, and take a break. Don't drink. Stuff bud in an olive and nibble away. Decoction of root used to induce emesis.*

Medicinal uses: Caustic plant juice applied to warts and a poultice of leaves applied to arthritic joints as a counterirritant.

MINT PEPPERMINT
Lamiaceae (*Mentha piperita, M. aquatica*)

Mentha aquatic

Identification: There are many American members of the mint family. The genus has several characteristics in common: a square stem, almost always aromatic when crushed, typically aggressive and spreading. Flowers are in dense whorls culminating in a terminal spike of blossoms that crown the stem, or in the leaf axils. Color varies by species—white, violet, blue. . . . The root is a spreading rhizome with erect stems. Leaves are ovate to roundish and elongated in a few species, typically serrated.

Habitat: *Mentha aquatic* and *M. piperita* can usually be found around water, shorelines, stream banks, dunes of the Great Lakes, and mountain passes, blow-downs, avalanche slides, and wet meadows.

Food uses: Leaves in teas, salads, cold drinks, sautéed vegetables; wonderful in Mexican bean soups, and as an integral part of the subcontinent and Middle Eastern flavor principles.

Medicinal uses: Leaf and flower infusion (or the extracted oil) are antiseptic, carminative, warming, and relieve muscle spasms and increase perspiration. Tea stimulates bile secretion. Leaf and flower extraction are Commission E–approved in Germany for treating dyspepsia and gallbladder and liver problems.

PICKERELWEED

Pontederiaceae (*Pontederia cordata*)

Identification: Arrow-shaped leaf, veins spread from base, merge at tip like venation in grass leaves; blue flowers, densely clustered spikes.

Habitat: Ponds and lakes in entire United States, except extreme desert, southern California, and lower Florida.

Food uses: Young leaves (before they emerge from the water), mature seeds and leaves eaten. Leaves are most tender in spring, while unfurling beneath water. Cook leaves with dandelions and mustard greens. Season cooked greens with Italian dressing or herbes de Provence; serve hot. Add flower petals to salads. In late summer seeds mature in tough, leathery capsules. Open capsule to get fruit. Munch as a trail food, or dry and grind into flour.

Medicinal uses: Infusion of whole plant historically used by 2 North American native tribes as a contraceptive. See Daniel Moerman, *Native American Ethnobotany*.

REED GRASS

Poaceae (*Phragmites communis*)

Identification: Tall wetland grass; lance-shaped leaves up to 1' in length; flowers in tall, dense plume. Plants grow in dense cluster. Found around the margins of streams and in wet lowlands. The root of reed grass, like cattail roots, harvested and leached of its starch.

Habitat: Wetlands throughout the United States.

Food uses: The first shoots of spring eaten raw but are best steamed until tender. I prefer to cut open the reed shoot to chew and suck the young shoots, then spit out the pulp. Prepare the plant immediately after picking, as delays in preparation make for a tough, stringy meal. Simply chop the new shoots into a manageable size and place them in a steamer. They are ready to eat in 5 minutes. In the fall, seeds ground into flour or stripped, crushed, and cooked with berries. Also, try reed seeds cooked in stews and soups.

Medicinal uses: The Chinese use plant to clear fevers, quench thirst, promote diuresis, and promote salivation.

Note: The dried, hollow stalks of reed cut to 4" lengths and used as spigots for tapping maple trees for syrup.

RICE, WILD
Poaceae (*Zizania aquatica, Z. palustris*)
Identification: Tall grass with a somewhat reedlike flower head; long, narrow leaf blades; flowers in tall plume; upper flowers female, lower flowers male.

Habitat: Wild rice found growing in shallow, clean, slow-moving water, east of the Missouri River.

Food uses: Seeds harvested in August and September. Timing is critical, so check your stand of wild rice often. Mature seeds drop off easily. Return every other day to maximize the harvest. Use a rolling pin to thresh the husks from the seed. Simply roll back and forth over the grain. Use a fan or the wind to dispel the chaff. *Cooking tips:* The simplest way to cook wild rice is to boil 2 cups of lightly salted water, add 1 cup of wild rice, and cover and simmer for 35 minutes. *Zizania* is an excellent stuffing for wild turkey. Wild rice, cooked until tender, is an excellent addition to pancake and waffle mixes. It also goes well in 12- and 20-grain hot cereals and is a great substitute for white rice. Extend your supply by cooking it with equal parts of long-grain brown rice.

Medicinal uses: Staple cereal crop for Native Americans, providing winter nutrition in a harsh climate.

SWAMP DOCK
Polygonaceae (*Rumex orbiculatus, R. crispus, R. patientia*)
I include all docks here, although *Rumex crispus* and *Rumex orbiculatus* are typically found along the edges of roadsides, in gardens, and meadows.

Identification: The many varieties of dock are common weeds growing on disturbed ground, edges of fields,

Swamp dock

roadsides, and vacant lots. Leaves typically widest at base, narrow to tip, rounded at base; paper-like flower spikes; fruits 3 parted, brownish to red with 3 nutlets. Docks emerge in the spring, first as unfurling leaves, later the flower spike shoots up with smaller leaves attached. Flowers and eventually seeds cluster along the top several inches of the spikes. Swamp or water dock (*R. orbiculatus*) is found growing in water or along stream margins. It is stout and tall (to 6') with a

Curly leaf dock

long root and flat, narrow, dark-green leaves. Both curly dock (*R. crispus*) and yellow dock (*R. patientia*) have curly or wavy leaf margins.

Habitat: Entire United States except arid areas, along streams, in marshes and wetlands.

> *Warning: Contains oxalic acid; like spinach, do not eat more than twice a week.*

Food uses: My favorite species is *R. crispus*. It grows in profusion in the garden and is available as food in March. Leaves and seeds edible; tender young leaves, as they emerge, are most edible. Older leaves are tough and bitter and must be cooked in 2 changes of water. Steam, sauté, or stir-fry young leaves, season with ginger, soy, lemon juice, and sesame seed oil. Leaves are great with walnuts and raisins. Dock seeds are edible in late summer and autumn. Hulled seeds can be ground into flour and used as a soup thickener or as a flour extender in baked goods.

Medicinal uses: Curly dock and yellow dock used by naturopaths and midwives as a tea to treat anemia and raise iron levels in pregnant women. Iron in this form does not cause constipation. Curly dock root also used with vinegar to treat ringworm. All dock roots are laxative, bitter digestive stimulants.

WATERCRESS

Brassicaceae (*Nasturtium officinale*)

Identification: Grows along the margins of shallow, clean water. Alternate leaves to ¾" wide, ovate, simple, broad near base; small white flower with 4 petals. Avoid contamination from pesticides and herbicides—collect watercress (and, for that matter, all edible water plants)

from a clean water source such as a highland stream or free-flowing spring.

Habitat: Throughout the United States, springs, free-flowing streams, with rich bottoms.

Food uses: Watercress is a pungent, spicy green. It's an important ingredient in V8 vegetable juice and one of the most useful greens known to humankind. In the northern United States and Canada, watercress is available 10 months a year. South of the Mason-Dixon Line, it's a year-round food. Watercress is high in vitamins A and C. Scramble chopped watercress with eggs, stuff a pita sandwich, add it to salads, or make watercress soup. I like to stir-fry watercress with 1 tablespoon of olive oil, 2 tablespoons of soy sauce, 1 tablespoon of lemon juice, 1 teaspoon of diced ginger root, and the juice of 1 pressed garlic clove. Cook briefly at medium heat for about 2 minutes. Use watercress as a stuffing when preparing smoked or baked bass. After washing the body cavity, stuff the fish with watercress, season to taste, and bake or smoke it. I like watercress as a wild ingredient on pizza.

Medicinal uses: Mild diuretic. A few Native American groups used watercress to dissolve gallstones.

YELLOW POND LILY, SPATTERDOCK
Scrophulariaceae (*Nuphar variegatum, N. luteum*)

Identification: These 2 closely related species found in ponds, shallow lakes, and streams. Their disk-shaped leaves unfurl above water. The yellow flower blooms through the summer and bears a primitive-looking fruit. The fruit pod contains numerous seeds—perhaps the only palatable part of this plant.

Habitat: Throughout the United States, except extreme mountain and desert regions. The Yellowstone National Park variety (long isolated) is about a third larger in size.

Food uses: The root stock of spatterdock is cut free and boiled. It smells sweet like an apple, but it is extremely bitter—even after cooking in 2 or 3 changes of water. Strictly a survival food; eat when nothing else is available. The seeds can be dried and ground into flour or prepared like popcorn. Place the dried seeds in a popcorn popper. Cover the machine so the small seeds don't become airborne. The results are usually disappointing. Seeds simply pop open, but they're edible with salt and butter.

Medicinal uses: Root poultice over wounds, swellings, boils, and inflammations. Root tea.

Edible Plants of Eastern Forested Areas

CLEAVERS, BEDSTRAW
Rubiaceae (*Galium aparine*)
Identification: Weak, slender stem; 8 leaves in whorl; tiny white flowers. Found in woodlands, along streams, and in vacant lots, often around the roots of hardwoods and other trees. Mature plant clings to clothing.

Habitat: Hardwood forests in eastern United States, roughly to the Mississippi, Ontario, and south to Florida.

Food uses: Also called bedstraw; add young cleaver leaves to salads in early spring. Mature leaves are tough and must be boiled and sautéed. Seeds of summer can be roasted and ground into coffee substitute. It's better than chicory but far short of coffee.

Medicinal uses: Diuretic. Tea used for skin diseases such as psoriasis, seborrhea, and eczema. Whole plant juice taken internally for kidney stones and cancer.

FALSE SOLOMON'S SEAL
Liliaceae (*Smilacina* sp.)
Identification: Solomon's seal has flower umbels in the notch of each leaf whereas false Solomon's seal has a flower spike at the top of the plant. This is a perennial with adventitious root stocks that produce the solitary stem, with alternating, lance-shaped leaves, partially clasping the stem; white flowers in a cluster at the top of the plant.

Habitat: Western United States in coniferous forest areas to 8,000', and in the eastern hardwood forests and shaded dune areas along the Great Lakes, north to Ontario, south to Kentucky and Tennessee.

Food uses: The young shoots of Solomon's seal are edible, but berries may be emetic. That is, they may cause you to vomit. Root stocks of false Solomon's seal are inedible unless precooked in lye to remove bitterness. Sample this plant judiciously. This is a beautiful herbal that needs little care and has a different look each season.

Medicinal uses: Buds infused to treat chronic conditions; little documentation available.

FERN, MAIDENHAIR
Polypodiaceae (*Adiantum pedatum*)
Identification: Shiny black (or dark-brown) wiry stems, supporting delicate leaflets; 15–40 leaflets per leaf, providing the appearance of a fan.

Habitat: Several species found from coast to coast, lowlands, coastal areas, and mountain areas, prefers shade and moisture.

Food uses: Fiddleheads are edible. Pick when tightly coiled; after unfurling, the fiddleheads and plant are inedible—a

marginal food, for survival use only. Steam fiddlehead, then sauté in oil or butter before eating.

Medicinal uses: Leaves of plant are styptic and applied to skin to stop bleeding. Leaf tea used to rinse hair.

GINGER, WILD
Aristolochiaceae (*Asarum canadense*)
Identification: Aromatic root, smells like ginger; 2 dark-green heart-shaped leaves; note the hairy stem and leaves; primitive flower emerging under the leaves in May in Michigan. Growing from a spreading, adventitious rhizome. Found on rich soil in moist woods as a spreading ground cover in shady areas.

Habitat: Various species grow across the entire United States, except extreme desert, southern California, and lower Florida.

Food uses: Crushed root added to salad dressings. When dried and grated it is an adequate substitute for Oriental ginger. For the daring gourmet, try boiling the root until tender and then simmer in maple syrup. The result is an unusual candy treat. Taste the leaves.

Medicinal uses: Root traditionally used to treat colds and cough; antiseptic and tonic. Herbalists use the root in tincture to dilate peripheral blood vessels; unproven.

GINSENG

Araliaceae (*Panax quinquefolius*)

Identification: Rare perennial. Straight, erect stem, with 2 or 3 leaf stems; typically 5 but up to 11 leaves per stem. The best place to find ginseng is in cultivation or at a botanical garden. Plant protected in most states, but you can order roots from Pacific Botanicals (pacificbotanicals.com) and other purveyors.

Dwarf ginseng

Habitat: Eastern United States, roughly to the Mississippi River in rich moist woods, well drained, in dark and dank places. The easier-to-find dwarf ginseng is more prevalent. Plant is cultivated in the East and West and readily available in various forms.

Food uses: American ginseng root, a prized medicinal in China, sells for about $300 per pound in markets there. Cook the root in chicken soup. Eat the berries. Dried root can be ground with an old-fashioned sausage grinder, then simmered in water as a pick-me-up. Add root slices to gin, vodka, bourbon to extract the virtues—it relieves the pressures of life!

Medicinal uses: Ginseng root's active ingredients, called saponins (glycosides) raise blood pressure, others lower it; some raise blood sugar, some lower it. Today saponins from ginseng show an anticancer chemotherapy in preliminary studies.

GROUNDNUT

Fabaceae (*Apios americana*)

Identification: Climbing, pealike plant vine; numerous tubers along length of root; leaves alternate, compound, feather-like; seeds in long pods, pealike.

Habitat: Groundnut grows on wet ground, along the fringes of streams, bogs, and thickets, climbing shrubs, twining its way toward the sun, in shoe-wetting and deeply shaded marshes. Easily transferred to your garden, where the root can be harvested in the autumn or spring. Found across the entire United States, except extreme desert, southern California, and lower Florida.

Food uses: Seeds are edible. Cook them like lentils. Tubers of *Apios* are 15 percent protein—a great potato substitute. Native Americans established settlements near this staple—a high-protein foraging food.

Medicinal uses: This is a case of your-food-is-your-medicine: Native Americans used the pealike, lentil-like seeds as survival food. Most eastern tribes ate the seeds and roots, without which in the winter they may have starved.

INDIAN CUCUMBER

Liliaceae (*Medeola virginiana*)
Identification: Ovate to lanceolate pointed leaves, typically 7 in a whorl around stem. Blue berries. Plant grows 5"–7" tall.

Habitat: Moist deciduous forest, found around the bases of oaks. Favorite place is the back entrance to Grand Mere State Park, Stevensville, Michigan.

Food uses: Indian cucumber root has an edible root tuber—root tastes cucumber-like—wash and eat raw. Gouge out of the ground with your fingers and eat fresh.

Medicinal uses: Whole plant infused and used externally on many skin ailments—considered a panacea by Native Americans. Berries used as an anticonvulsive. Dried leaves and berries given to youngsters and babies in infusion. Root tea also used as a diuretic to treat congestive heart failure.

JACK-IN-THE-PULPIT, INDIAN TURNIP
Araceae (*Arisaema triphyllum*)

Identification: Leaves compound, 3 leaflets, oval, smooth, lighter underside; distinctive primitive flower, spadix in pulpit-like spathe.

Habitat: Found in rich soils, generally woods or shady lowland, with skunk cabbage and mayapple nearby. Found across the entire United States, except extreme desert, southern California, and lower Florida.

Food uses: Native Americans sliced roots and dried them, deactivating calcium oxalate. Dried root was cooked twice (boiled and then sautéed) and eaten like potato chips. I consider this a survival foot—eat to survive, not to thrive.

Warning: Do not eat fresh plant. Like skunk cabbage and mayapple, Jack-in-the-pulpit contains caustic oxalates when fresh; thoroughly dry before use. Not recommended. Handle with care: Calcium oxalate will cause painful burns in cracked skin or open sores. See also Appendix A: Poisonous Plants.

Medicinal uses: Plant parts used to treat cough, sore throat, ringworm, and as a poultice for boils and abscesses.

MARSH MARIGOLD, COWSLIP
Ranunculaceae (*Caltha palustris* and other *Caltha* species)

Identification: Leaves ovate on yellow-green stems; distinctive fluorescent-yellow flowers.

Habitat: Thrives in sunlight to partial shade. Plants grow in low wetlands often in large colonies, in marshes, along stream edges and wet fields, often with roots submerged in water. Found across the entire United States, except extreme desert, southern California, and lower Florida.

Food uses: Leaves eaten as a potherb in the spring before the flowers open (cook twice, boil them, sauté, then do it all again). Cooking in several changes of water denatures the caustic alkaloid. Actually, leaves are extremely bitter and not worth the time and trouble. So why do I put it here? This lovely plant is worth your attention.

Warning: In view of the caustic nature of this plant, use it as a survival food only.

Medicinal uses: Leaves used as laxative and cough syrup. Root used in decoction for colds.

RAMPS, WILD LEEKS
Liliaceae (*Allium tricoccum*)

Identification: Strong onion aroma; long, wide leaves grow directly from bulb on short stem. Leaves are transient, gone from the plant in 3 or 4 weeks, giving rise to a flowering stem and white flowers. By July all that is evident of the plant is a stem with shiny black seeds. Bulb is still there, so dig.

Habitat: Eastern United States, roughly to the Mississippi River. Found on banks in wet woods, above seeps, on rich and moist hillsides, deciduous forest, especially beech-maple climax woods.

Food uses: Leaves, stems, and bulbs are edible—marvelous in stews and soup, or sautéed with soy sauce, extra-virgin olive oil, and a little water to keep plants from sticking to pan. For a martini treat, stuff fresh bulbs in large olives, drop olives in martini. Did I mention pizza? Delicious—and an absolute must in tomato sauce.

Medicinal uses: Used as a tonic to combat colds. Disputed evidence suggests eating raw bulbs may reduce risk of heart disease. Chop leaves into chicken soup to potentiate this cold and flu fighter.

RUE ANEMONE, WOOD ANEMONE
Ranunculaceae (*Thalictrum thalictroides*)

Identification: The windflower is a member of the buttercup family with small and delicate lobed leaves (that shake in the lightest breeze, thus the common name). Perennial grows to 8", has a white flower with 6 petals, and is an early bloomer, April, typically in Michigan; sooner in Kentucky and Tennessee. Root consists of 2, 3, or 4 attached tubers.

Habitat: Found on the floor of hardwood forests of the East, in well-drained soil, scattered here and there over the ground.

Warning: Potentially toxic; avoid this plant as a foodstuff. I include this plant here because of its extensive availability. You will find it and become curious, but try it at your own risk.

Food uses: I have eaten these peppery roots in small quantities. Starchy root said to be edible after cooking, but most members of the buttercup family are toxic; regardless of what other field guides may say, I recommend you do not eat this root.

Medicinal uses: Cherokee used a tea of the root to stem diarrhea. Root tea also used to stem vomiting.

SOLOMON'S SEAL

Liliaceae (*Polygonatum biflorum*)

Identification: Rising from an adventitious root (where the previous year's growth leaves a seal-like scar), a single stalk with lance-shaped leaves with buds and flowers in the notches (leaf axils) of the leaves. Flowers greenish white, bell shaped, producing a blue-black berry.

Habitat: Hardwood forests from the East Coast to Nebraska, north to Ontario and south to Louisiana, Florida, and Texas.

Food uses: Starchy rhizomes used as food; must be cooked. Young shoot of Solomon's seal are fair as a trail food steamed or cooked with mixed vegetables.

> *Warning: Sample judiciously. Large quantities may be harmful. Berries considered poisonous. I have nibbled on a few and am still here (though some would say my mind is gone).*

Medicinal uses: Purchase sliced and dried roots of Chinese Solomon's seal in Chinese supermarkets. The root is rich in polysaccharides and considered antidiabetic. Cook the store-purchased Chinese variety in stir-fry or in noodle soups. *Polygonatum* root used by holistic practitioners and Native Americans, sliced and infused in water to treat indigestion, excessive menstruation, and exhaustion. Cold wine root infusion used in Spanish medicine, used as a with arnica tincture to clear or prevent bruises.

SPRING BEAUTY

Portulacaceae (*Claytonia caroliniana*)
Indian Potato (*C. lanceolata*)
Mountain Potato (*C. tuberosa*)

Identification: Approximately 7" tall; narrow lance-shaped leaves die off after bloom; flowers 1 centimeter across, light pink to white or white with pink veins, in loose terminal clusters, numbering 3–18. Plant grows from ground where it is attached to an acorn-size, fleshy corm (oval or globular stem base swollen with food and water surrounded by papery scale). Emerges and blooms in early spring.

Habitat: Found in rich, moist woods throughout the East and across the northern tier of United States and the mountainous West, on wooded stream banks. Entire United States, except extreme desert, southern California, lower Florida, and the prairie states.

Food uses: The brown-skinned corm is edible. Peel the skin, wash, and eat raw or cooked. Try it on the grill with roasted vegetables. Roll the corm in olive oil, and then roast for about 8 minutes until browned. Flowers are edible but bland. Young leaves boiled for 10 minutes and eaten, but poor tasting. The real beauty of this plant is in the eyes of the beholder—as a foodstuff it's best left alone.

Medicinal uses: Tea from root used to reduce fever. Crushed leaves used as poultice over ulcers.

SWEET CICELY, WILD ANISE
Apiaceae (*Osmorhiza odorata* and other *Osmorhiza* species)
Identification: Perennial with slightly thickened roots, often in a cluster. Broken root smells like anise. Plant to 3' tall with bright green to greenish, shiny leaves; small greenish-white flowers in umbels (hemlock-like).

Habitat: Typically, hardwood forest (shaded or partially shaded), often found around the bases of trees, located in the entire United States, except extreme desert, southern California, and lower Florida.

> *Warning: Looks like poison hemlock. First-time foragers, collect only with an expert. Find an expert at your county or state park. They give wild plants talks and walks.*

Food uses: Wild anise, commonly called sweet cicely, has a sweet anise odor and taste. Use as an anise substitute to spice cooked greens. Leaves added to salads.

Medicinal uses: Leaves occasionally eaten by diabetics as sugar substitute.

TOOTHWORT, CUT-LEAF

Brassicaceae (*Dentaria laciniata*)

Identification: Perennial to 6", with deeply cut leaflets, typically 5 lobed leaflets per leaf, 3 compound leaves in a whorl around plant. Flower blue-white to pinkish. Early spring bloomer, often in dense colonies.

Habitat: Hardwood forests of the East, from Ontario to Georgia, Maine to Iowa. Shade dwelling, typically found under oaks, beech, and maple. Blooms April through May.

Food uses: A favorite cooked green of the Cherokee, cut-leaf toothwort has an edible flower and edible root. I have not used this plant much. I like to munch on the flowers in the spring while fly casting on Volinia Creek near Dowagiac, Michigan.

Medicinal uses: Root used to treat toothache. Chew the root. Root also chewed for colds, flu. A decoction or tea of the root is used to clear the throat of phlegm or for treating sore throats as a gargle. Root chew also reported to treat hoarseness. The chewed root placed as a poultice over the head and temples to treat headache.

TRILLIUM, WHITE

Liliaceae (*Trillium grandiflorum*)

Identification: Leaves, sepals, and flower petals in threes. Blanket eastern woods in spring.

Habitat: Deciduous forest in East, shade to partial shade, typically in a mature woods, such as a beech-maple climax forest. Various species found in entire United States, except extreme desert, southern California, and lower Florida.

Trillium

Food uses: There are several varieties of trillium. The leaves and white, red, and purple flowers are edible, but for my taste, members of this genus are too pretty to eat. Trillium and toadshade (a red-flowered species) are easy to grow in the home garden. Locate in shade and rich soil.

Toadshade

Medicinal uses: Native Americans used *Trillium grandiflorum* root bark decoction for ear sores, and splinters of wood soaked in root extraction and then pricked through the skin over arthritic joints to relieve pain.

TROUT LILY

Liliaceae (*Erythronium americanum*)
Identification: Yellow-flowered trout lily has mottled, shiny leaves and a small, yellow, lily-like flower. 6"–8" tall, often sub-arboreal (around bases of hardwoods in East) in colonies that may blanket the forest floor. Avalanche lilies (of the mountainous West) are close relatives with edible bulbs.

Habitat: Moist forest floor, around the bases of hardwoods, often in dense colonies. Various species both east and west of the Mississippi River, from the East Coast to the coastal mountains of the West.

Warning: Plant protected in many states.

Food uses: Young leaves boiled and sautéed, with unremarkable results. Tuber after boiling may be sliced and eaten.

Medicinal uses: Root infusion used to reduce fevers. Crushed leaves used as a moist poultice over wounds and irritations.

VIOLETS, WOODLAND

Violaceae (*Viola* spp.)
Violets are cultivated in France for perfume. This incredible edible is high in vitamins A, C, and E.
Identification: Flower irregular; leaves vary, usually ovate; common blue violet has heart-shaped, serrated leaves—a volunteer found in shady areas along fringes of lawn.

Habitat: Yellow- and white-flowered violets as well as bird's-foot violets are found in eastern woods and montane areas of the West, coast to coast in forested areas, lowlands, and mountains. They prefer moist forests, conifers, or hardwoods.

Warning: Late-season plants without flowers can be confused with inedible greens. Forage this plant only when in bloom.

Violets east and west

Food uses: Use both the leaves and flowers in salads. Flowers may be candied—dissolve sugar into alcohol, brush on hypertonic solution, and let crystalize. Experiment! Put them over finished meat dishes as a garnish and color contrast that invites eating. I like plucking the flowers and munching them as I hike through the forest.

Medicinal uses: Violet roots consumed in large amounts are emetic and purgative. Plant used as poultice over skin abrasions. In China indigenous healthcare givers use one species, *V. diffusa,* to treat aplastic anemia, leukemia, mastitis, mumps, and venomous snakebites. The violet's color suggests the

Bird's foot violet

presence of anthocyanin, secondary metabolites that give off a blue hue. Anthocyanin also provides protection from *E. coli* infection.

Trees and Nuts

ALDER

Betulaceae (*Alnus* spp.)

Identification: These members of the birch family grow to 80', often much smaller. Bark smooth and gray when young, gets coarse and whitish gray when mature. The bark on *Alnus rubra* turns red to orange when exposed to moisture. Leaves are bright green, oval, coarsely toothed, and pointed. Male flowers are clustered in long hanging catkins; female seed capsule is ovoid cone; seed nuts small, slightly winged, and flat.

Habitat: Alder prefers moist areas. Species range from California to Alaska east to Idaho. Numerous species found across North America, often in impenetrable mazes surrounding streambeds—great bear habitat; be careful.

Food uses: Members of this genus provide a generous resource of firewood in the Northwest for savory barbecue cooking. Smoking helps preserve meat. Soak meat in a salt brine, then smoke. The bark and wood chips are preferred over mesquite for smoking fish, especially salmon. Scrape sweet inner bark (in the early spring) and eat raw, or combine with flour to make cakes.

Medicinal uses: Sweat-lodge floors were often covered with alder leaves, and switches of alder were used for applying water to the body and the hot rocks. Alder ashes used as a paste and applied with an alder chewing stick to clean teeth. Cones of subspecies *A. sinuata* used as medicine, as are other alder species. Spring catkins smashed to pulp and eaten as a cathartic (help move bowels). The bark mixed with other plants in decoction and used as a tonic. The decoction of the female catkins used to treat gonorrhea. A poultice of leaves applied to skin wounds and skin infections. In the Okanagan area of central Washington and British Columbia, First People used an infusion of new end shoots, new plant tops as an appetite stimulant for children. Leaf tea infusion said to be itch- and inflammation-relieving wash for insect bites and stings, poison ivy, and poison oak. Upper Tanana informants reported a decoction of the inner bark reduces fever. Infusion of bark used to wash sores, cuts, and wounds. This is still an important "warrior plant" in sweat-lodge ceremonies, a cleansing spiritual rite. For more on sweat lodges, see the DVD *Native American Medicine* at herbvideos.com.

Notes: Smoking meat with alder: Wood chips are soaked overnight in water, then placed on coals or charcoal to smoke meat. In 1961 I saw more than 100 Native Americans smoking fish, moose, and caribou for winter storage along a 10-mile stretch of the Denali Highway in Alaska. Local hunting rules then required any person who shot a caribou was obliged to give some of the meat to the First People, who preserved it for winter food. Fish flayed, stabbed through with a stick, and hung from wood weirs above a smoldering alder fire until smoked and dry. In hardwood-poor areas of the West, red alder burns slower than pine and is a suitable home-heating fuel. Bark may be stripped and soaked in water to make an orange to rust-colored dye.

BEECH TREE, AMERICAN BEECH

Fagaceae (*Fagus grandifolia*)

Identification: Tall (to 160') tree; leaves alternate, toothed, straight, and parallel veined, short stalked; bark light gray and smooth; twigs slender with long narrow scaly buds. Beechnut fruit (to ¾" long) is in a spiny husk, meat protected by a tough shell—fruits fall in late summer.

Habitat: Climax species in eastern forests. Beech and hard maple end the process of succession in hardwood forests. Prefers rich soil, open forest. Chemical in plant kills most understory competitors.

Food uses: Years ago hogs roamed the eastern forests eating the nuts. Quite a feat, as the nuts, encased in a durable husk, then a shell, leave little room for meat. Tasty though. Squirrels will get to the nuts before you can. Watch a squirrel in a beech forest—it may lead you to a cache of hundreds of nuts. Good luck.

Medicinal uses: Bark decoction taken to induce abortions, also used for pulmonary problems. Leaves decocted and compressed as a poultice over wounds and sores. Leaf decoction also used over burns. Nuts eaten to treat worms, much the same as pumpkin seeds.

BUTTERNUTS

Juglandaceae (*Juglans cinerea*)

Identification: Grows to 120'; round top, smooth bark; light-gray young branches, becoming light brown and deeply fissured. Buds dark brown, ovoid, and flattened; leaves to 25" long and shorter, with stout petioles, compound with 11–17 oblong lance-shaped leaflets, 2"–4" long; thick-husked fruit in clusters, nut elongated as compared to a walnut.

Habitat: Southwestern Michigan stretches the northern limit of this eastern tree, from New Brunswick to Alabama, Virginia to South Dakota; more abundant in the North. Tolerates drier climates, but prefers rich, moist banks near streams and rivers.

Food uses: Biggest of the walnut family; spoils easily, however. Collect butternuts from ground, throw them in water; those that sink are worth opening. Floating nuts have had an adventurous creature in them eating the nut meat. Native Americans crushed and ground nut meats to paste as a baby food.

Medicinal uses: Juglone, in the bark, root, and seed hulls, is anticancer, antimicrobial, cathartic, and antiparasitic. Native Americans used bark decoction to treat diarrhea and as a purgative, and an infusion of buds to treat mouth sores, mouth ulcers, and cleanse breath.

CHESTNUT

Fagaceae (*Castanea dentata*)

Identification: American chestnut, to 180', round topped with horizontal limbs; mature branches dark brown, yellow green when young. Leaves oblong to lance shaped, with short petioles, leaves shiny green turning yellow in the fall. Nut shell covered with numerous spines, opens with first frost to bear shelled nut. Chestnuts found in botanical gardens and secret hideaways. More common is the Chinese chestnut. Do not confuse these trees with the buckeye or horse chestnut. Chestnuts may be removed from their spiny husk, then crack the protecting shell and eat fresh whole, sliced, as a meal (ground), or roasted. Try them roasted in stuffing for goose, turkey, duck, or chicken.

Habitat: Throughout eastern United States, from Maine to Florida, east to Ontario and the Mississippi River. Prefers moist forest and thrives on a variety of soils.

Food uses: Native Americans dried then ground chestnuts and used the meal to make bread. I like it in gravies, stuffing, cooked in a soup. Try roasting the nuts, then grinding them and making coffee. *Tamale masa* made with ground chestnut and cornmeal—delicious. I like them mashed to meal, then mixed with dried currants and dried cranberries and cooked in my 7-grain hot cereal. Nut meats are delicious in potato soups, corn soups, and various chowders. Try them added to hominy or mixed in corn bread. Smash a few nuts and mix them in sweet potato soup or mashed potatoes.

COCONUT PALM, COCOS

Arecaceae (*Cocos nucifera*)

Identification: The coconut palm is a long-lived plant (100 years), has a single trunk, 70'–90' tall, bark is smooth and gray, marked by ringed scars left by fallen palm leaf. Leaves, 12'–20' long, pinnate; consisting of linear-lanceolate, more or less recurved, rigid, bright-green leaflets. Flower arising at leaf axils and enveloped by a spathe. Flowers bear lance-shaped petals, 6 stamens, and an ovary consisting of 3 connate carpels. Fruit 2½–5 pounds in weight and as big as a human head.

Habitat: The coconut palm thrives on sandy, saline soils; it requires abundant sunlight and regular rainfall; often located just above the tidal zone along tropical and subtropical beaches—transplant to yards and gardens in same climate.

Food uses: Soft fresh endosperm (milk and soft meat) used to feed infants when mother's milk not available—often mixed with bananas. Hispanics mix corn water and soy milk with the coconut milk as a nutritious food for infants and children. Coconut milk said to prevent curdling of milk in infants. Coconut meat is nutritious and eaten raw, cooked, shredded, or sweetened.

Medicinal uses: Coconut oil used cosmetically on the skin. Hawaiian people use this as a complete body lotion, excellent for massage. Inhaling smoke from burning the fruit shells said to induce abortion. Meat rubbed on the head as a brain tonic and dried ash of meat eaten as a tonic. Endosperm considered a good food for diabetics if unsweetened. In Mexican medicine meat and milk thought useful for treating diarrhea, dysentery, colitis, gastritis, indigestion, ulcers, and hepatitis. Meat and endosperm milk considered a tonic, used to rehabilitate the physically weak. Soft flesh rubbed on acne, wrinkles; oil is a good moisturizing cosmetic lotion. Coconut milk taken with lime juice is a refrigerant (cooling), rehydrates children and adults, and lowers acidity of urine.

HAZELNUT

Betulaceae (*Corylus cornuta*)

Identification: Tall shrubs or small trees with leaves to 5", coarse, toothed (double toothed). Nuts in a bristly husk. Often found as understory, rich soil preferred, along edges of woods, fens, and marshes.

Habitat: Beaked hazelnut is abundant in southern Michigan and Washington State—where they are cultivated. Wild strains found here and there and in between.

Food uses: You have to beat the squirrels to these, favorite nut of the fox squirrel. Remove husk, roast, and eat. Not bad raw. Nuts can be ground into nut flour; great nutritional boost to bread, pancakes, and waffles. Try cooking nuts in soups and stews and with game. Hazelnut bread is popular in Washington. Nuts dipped in honey and roasted—messy and delicious.

Medicinal uses: Native Americans infused branches and leaves to treat intestinal disorders and heart trouble. Boiled bark used to induce emesis.

HICKORY, SHAGBARK
Juglandaceae (*Carya ovata*)
Identification: Tall tree, 60'–90', with 5–7 hairless leaflets; compound leaves 8"–14" in length. Light-colored shedding bark indicative, often peeling (shagging) away from tree in long, narrow sheets. Buds covered with overlapping scales. Nuts egg shaped in thick yellow husk splitting to base.

Habitat: In deciduous forests of East, north to the Upper Peninsula of Michigan, south to the Gulf Coast states excluding Florida, west to the plains, and east to the coast.

Food uses: Tree tapped for sap makes a unique and savory syrup, with the flavor of hickory nuts. Nuts are edible and splendid—sweet and succulent, only surpassed by butternut. Use in salads, syrups, on pancakes and waffles, and everywhere a superior nut flavor is desired.

Note: Husking and shelling nuts is difficult work but worth the effort. I purchase mine (shelled) from an Amish family for about $6 a pint. I cannot do it that cheap.

Medicinal uses: Small shoots of spring steamed as a respiratory inhalant for congestion and headaches. Spring shoots placed on hot stones in sweat lodges for soothing inhalant. Bark boiled and decoction sipped to treat arthritis—this hot bark infusion considered a panacea, treatment for general malaise as a tonic.

LARCH, TAMARACK
Pinaceae (*Larix laricina*)
Identification: Medium to large wetlands tree of the North; at first appearance it looks like a typical pine or fir, needles slender to 1" in length emanating from short spurs on branch, in clusters, single or several, with nondrooping branch (whereas European larch has drooping branches); cones less than ¾" in length, almost round; bark flakes off in scales. Unlike pine and fir, larch is deciduous and loses its needles through the winter.

Habitat: Wetlands of the North, West, and Northwest, and along stream banks—prevalent along the South Shore Trail of Hyalite Reservoir in Montana. Bald cypress, a similar species, found in wet areas of the southern United States.

Food uses: Tender new shoots infused into tea or pan-fried as food. The inner bark can be scraped, dried, and pounded into flour; reconstitute with water and make flat bread.

Medicinal uses: Native Americans used the bark extraction and balsam (resin) of the plant in combination with other plants in decoction to treat acute infections such as colds, flu, fever, coughs. Various tribes utilized the bark infusion of young shoots as a laxative. Bark and wood poultice used to treat wounds and draw out infection. Inner bark infusion considered warming. The resinous balsam used as a stimulating inhalant. Leaves and bark were pounded, crushed, and used as a poultice to reduce headache. This ritual sweat-lodge plant is useful for relieving tension, backache, and headache. Needles, twig, bark wetted and applied to hot stones to produce steam. Western larch, *Larix occidentalis,* found west of the plains states and used in similar ways to include the decoction of the new growth as a wash for cancer. The resinous pitch of the western species mixed with animal fat and used on wounds, cuts, and burns. *Larix decidua,* tamarack's European cousin, is Commission E–approved for treating coughs, colds, bronchitis, and fever, and to promote resistance to acute infections.

Notes: This rot-resistant relative of cypress is used to make long-lived railroad ties. The tree's tough, fibrous, and rot-resistant roots make good sewing and basket-weaving material and were often used to sew birch bark together to make canoes. Shredded inner bark fed to horses.

MADRONE

Ericaceae (*Arbutus menziesii*)

Identification: Evergreen, broadleaf tree growing along the seacoast of the Northwest. Young bark is chartreuse and smooth, whole. Older bark is dark brown to red and peeling. Evergreen leaves are alternate, oval, 7" long, shiny, dark green above, lighter, whitish green beneath, hairless, and leathery. White flowers that are urn shaped to 3" long in large drooping clusters. Fruit an orange-red berry about ½" across, with a granular skin.

Habitat: Typically found in coastal areas of northern California, Oregon, offshore islands of Washington and British Columbia, in typically dry, sunny areas with a sea exposure.

Food uses: Vancouver Salish used reddish bark in decoction when cooking to dye edible camas bulbs pink. Berries cooked before eating. Also, they were stored after steaming, dried, and reconstituted in hot water before eating. Berries smashed and made into a cider-like drink. Cider claimed by Miwok as an appetite stimulant and said to resolve upset stomach. Berries are also dried and stored for later use.

Medicinal uses: Saanich and other nations used bark and leaves for treating colds, tuberculosis, to treat stomach problems, and as a postpartum contraceptive. Decoctions of plant were also used as an emetic (Concow nation), which belays one from imbibing nonchalantly. Leaves used by Cowichan of Northwest as a burn treatment, dressing. Leaf infusion used to treat stomach ulcers. Also, fresh leaves eaten off tree for relieving cramps. Chewed leaves said to relieve sore throat (chew, swallow juice, but don't swallow leaves). Leaf infusion used by Skokomish to treat colds and treat ulcers. Bark infusion used to treat diarrhea. Bark decoction used for washing sores, wounds, impetigo; said to be astringent. Bark decoction also used as a gargle for sore throat, according to Pomo and Kashaya. Karok used leaves in puberty ceremony.

Notes: The wood was used to make canoes, and the berries are used as steel-head trout bait. Berries also dried and used as beads when making bracelets and necklaces.

MAPLE, SUGAR

Aceraceae (*Acer saccharum*)

Identification: Leaves have the basic form of Canada's national emblem. Crowns of trees are broad and rounded in the open. Bark is smooth when young and furrows with age. Leaves are typically 3 lobed. Seeds have the characteristic helicopter-blade appearance and fly accordingly.

Habitat: Climax species in eastern forests with beech. Trees found from Ontario south to Tennessee and west to eastern parts of South Dakota, Nebraska, Kansas, and Oklahoma.

Food uses: The seeds are eaten but are poor tasting. Pluck the seeds from the helicopter-blade husk and cook like peas, or stir-fry. You will soon have your fill of them. Maple sugar and maple syrup from the winter and spring sap are what these trees are all about. A maple sugar mill near you has taps or information as to where to purchase them (they'll probably sell or give you a few). Use a brace and ⅜" bit to drill through the bark until you hit hardwood. Clean the hole thoroughly, and then use a hammer to drive in the tap. Sap flows best on warm, sunny days after a freezing night. Tapping begins in late January and continues until the sap runs dark, thick, and stingy in early April. With trees under 10" wide, use only 1 tap. For larger trees, drive 2 or 3 taps in a circle around the tree. Use a covered pail to collect the sap. If you are going to boil the sap down on an open fire, make certain your wood is dry and presents very little smoke. Smoke will give an undesirable flavor to the syrup. I use 3 pans over a long and narrow fire pit. I pour the sugar water from pan to pan as it cooks. Pan number 1 receives the fresh water from the trees, pan 2 will receive the reduced water from pan 1, and pan 3 receives the further-reduced water from pan 2. Pan 3 of course will have the thickest, richest water. Boil the syrup in pan 3 until it coats a spoon.

Medicinal uses: Maple syrup is a glucose-rich sugar substitute with the added benefit of numerous minerals. I prefer it as a sweetener rather than refined sugar, which has no minerals. Traditionally, maple syrup was used to flavor and sweeten cough syrups. The unfinished fresh sap is considered a mineral-rich tonic. I store a couple gallons in the freezer and keep one in the refrigerator as a flavorful and nutritious water source.

Note: Other trees tapped for sap: black walnut, white, black, and yellow birch. Grape-vine canopy can be cut (to save the tree) in the spring, and they will provide copious amounts of mineral-laden water.

OAKS AND ACORNS
Fagaceae (*Quercus* spp.)

Identification: This is a large genera with species worldwide. I prefer the acorns from oaks that have rounded instead of pointed leaf lobes. White oak (*Quercus alba*) and bur oak are good examples from the eastern United States. Chinkapin oak also has sweet acorns. *Quercus alba* has white-gray

White oak

bark; evenly lobed hairless leaves 3"–9" (7–11 lobes, not pointed) and twigs that are also hairless. Acorn cup (cap) is bowl shaped covering one-third or less of acorn. Bur oak (*Q. macrocarpa*) is a tall tree (to 180') with leaves marked by deep indentations (1 or 2), dividing the leaves into 2 or more proportions. Leaves leathery and shiny above, hairy and whitish underneath. Acorn cups bowl shaped, with mossy (bur) fringe of elongated scales. Bark light gray, shallow grooved. Leaves 4"–10".

Bur oak

Habitat: Varieties of oaks are found throughout the United States: eastern forests, montane areas, California, Texas, New Mexico, Washington State. Bur oak, white oak, black oak, chinkapin, and red oaks are distributed throughout forests of the eastern United States.

Food uses: Oaks with leaves that are pointed have more tannins, and the acorns are too bitter to consume even after soaking in water. The best way to get acquainted with oaks and learn how to identify them is to visit an arboretum where oaks are labeled and identification is facilitated. Armed with this visual proof, you will be successful gathering nuts for the winter. White oak and bur oaks have sweet nut meat. Tannins in acorn meat embitter the taste. Tannins are water-soluble phenolic compounds that leach away in water, thus a water bath sweetens the nut. A quick fix in the kitchen is to puree the acorn meat in water. Use a blender and combine 1 cup of water with every cup of nut meat. Blend thoroughly. Press the water out of the nut meat through a clean pair of pantyhose, cheesecloth, or white sock. Keep in mind that a dirty white sock imparts an objectionable flavor to the nut meats. I like the acorn puree on baked potatoes, over tomato sauce, in all baking recipes, or out of hand as a snack.

Medicinal uses: White oak has tannin-rich bark. Tannins are antiseptic and astringent. Native Americans and pioneers made a tea from the bark for mouth sores, burns, cuts, and scrapes. The bark considered by many a panacea. We now know that tannins in oak and tea may provide cancer protection and are under investigation. Native Americans used bark tea for treating fevers and hives. Bark tea is astringent.

PECAN
Juglandaceae (*Carya illinoinensis*)
Identification: Leaflets 9–17 per leaf. End buds to 1" long with 2–3 pairs of non-overlapping yellow hairy bud scales, twigs hairless, bark closely ridged and nonpeeling. Hybrids have much bigger nut meats than wild types and grow to 160' in height. Nuts longer than wide, edible.

Habitat: This fertile-soil, bottomland dweller where temperatures are moderate and there is ample humidity, may not bear fruit for 20 years. Typically found wild along the Mississippi River, more on the west side.

Food uses: Lammes pecan chewies are my wife's favorites and may be purchased online or in Austin, Texas. I use pecans in salads, Paleo waffles, pancakes, cookies, candy, and with ham and vegetable dishes. The nut was stored for winter use.

Medicinal uses: Kiowa used a decoction of the bark to treat tuberculosis. Leaves crushed and rubbed over ringworm.

WHITE PINE AND PINYON PINE
Pinaceae (*Pinus strobus, Pinus edulis*)
Identification: White pine grows to over 100' and displays 5 needles in clusters, typically each with a white stripe on the side; they are 3 sided, 2½"–5" long. Branches form a whorl around trunk, and the age of the tree is

determined by the number of whorls. Pinecones are elongated with flexible scales. Pinyon pine grows to 20', with brown cones, typically in pairs, that are 2"–4" long. Seeds are up to ½" in length, inside a shell.

Habitat: White pine, because of its utility, found throughout the East and as an ornamental in many western states. Pinyon pine prefers a drier climate and grows at higher altitudes in the Mountain West—especially prevalent in the Four Corners area.

Food uses: White pine needles are made into tea. Take a handful of needles, crush them, and add them to a gallon jar of water containing mountain mint, lemon thyme, and lemon balm, then squeeze in juice of ½ lemon and let infuse in refrigerator for 6 hours. Uplifting! Seeds from both white and pinyon pine eaten. Pinyon pine is the premier edible seed (pine nuts) and is mashed to a paste and mixed with berries and spices for an unusual candy treat. Seeds on all pines are edible, but many are too small to effectively gather.

Medicinal uses: Pine pitch used to seal wounds, and it is antiseptic and disinfectant.

REDBUD TREE, EASTERN REDBUD

Leguminoceae (*Cercis canadensis*)

Identification: Small tree to 30', broad, open, and flat or rounded crown. Bark thin and gray on young stems; on older trees bark darkens to reddish brown to black, forming lone narrow scaly ridges; inner bark red. Leaves alternate, simple, heart shaped, dark green above and paler beneath. Flowers April to May, irregular, light-rose colored, pealike flowers, blooming before leaves open.

Habitat: Southwestern Michigan and south, through the southern states. Understory tree of forests and stream borders in moist ground. Associated with elm, basswood, silver maple, red ash, mulberry, and hackberry. Shade tolerant.

Redbud and pod

Food uses: I eat the flowers in spring and a little later, the young fruiting bodies. The flowers are tart and go well in salads, pancakes, fruit dishes. The pods (a fruiting legume) best dipped in a batter and cooked tempura-style.

Medicinal uses: Native Americans used the inner bark and root for respiratory congestion, pulmonary congestion, whooping cough. According to Duke in his *Handbook of Northeastern Indian Medicinal Plants,* the Delaware nation used the inner bark infusion to prevent vomiting and to reduce fevers.

SASSAFRAS

Lauraceae (*Sassafras albidum*)

Identification: Small to medium tree with mitten-shaped leaves (and other diverse shapes), aromatic leaves and twigs. The root is fragrant and smells a bit like root beer. Flowers are yellow-green.

Habitat: Found in eastern forests, often along the edges of woods and roadsides. It is a first growth in oak-hickory forests.

Food uses: Dried leaves of spring used as filé in gumbo. Crush the dried leaves of spring to powder and use as a spice. Also, spread the leaf powder on pasta, soup, cheese, and other savory dishes. For root tea, peel the root before you boil it.

Medicinal uses: Bark decoction used as a stimulant, pain reliever, astringent, and folk treatment for rheumatism. Safrole (found in leaves, roots, and bark) is touted to have a wide variety of medicinal uses including treatment of scurvy, skin sores, kidney problems, toothaches, rheumatism, swelling, menstrual disorders, and sexually transmitted diseases, bronchitis, hypertension, and dysentery.

> *Warning: The root oil used as an antiseptic until 1960 when USDA declared it unsafe because of the content of safrole, a carcinogenic toxin. There are no proven effects as a medicine, and because of the toxic effects of safrole, the plant extracts should not be eaten. That said, I chew the end twigs for flavor.*

Notes: When camping, use twigs as a toothbrush (chew stick). Chew the end of the twig until it is bristly, and then use the bristles to clean between your teeth. Extracts are used to make perfume and root beer.

WALNUT, BLACK

Juglandaceae (*Juglans nigra*)

Identification: 50'–90' in height and 2'–3' in diameter with a straight, clear trunk and narrow crown. Twigs and branches are thick. Leaves alternate, pinnately compound, 12"–24" long, with 10–24 sharply oval, finely toothed, long-pointed leaflets 3"–3½" long; bright, clear yellow in autumn. Flowers are yellow-green; males in catkins 2½"–5½" long; females on short spikes near twig ends. Fruit round, 2"–2½" across, with a thick, green, nonsplitting husk; nut inside is furrowed and hard; matures in late summer to fall.

Habitat: Deep, well-drained soils; grows best in rich bottomlands, moist coves, and streamsides; grows best on the lower north- or east-facing slopes.

Food uses: In baked goods, cereals, waffles, pancakes, salads. Or eat it on the hoof out of hand. This is a daily requirement in morning oatmeal. Try crushed black walnuts mixed in maple syrup.

Notes: To remove the husk (stain-producing covering of the walnut), you may put them on a paved driveway and roll them under your shoe. Or jack up a car slightly (about 1") off the ground, engage the transmission, and let the walnuts shoot under the tire. Some people wear gloves and use a hammer to pound and tug the husk away. Before shelling, drop unshelled walnuts in a bucket of water—those that float have worms that have eaten the nut meat. Open only the ones that sink.

Medicinal uses: Cholesterol-reducing in Loma Linda University test where participants ate 20 percent of their daily calories from walnuts. Diet also, ratio of LDL/HDL lowered by 12 percent (see *Nutrition Today,* vol. 30. No. 4, pp. 75–176; 1995). Walnuts may help prevent hyperthyroidism, scabies; may lessen inflammation of psoriasis and arthritis. Walnuts are rich in serotonin, mood-enhancing chemistry, and they may improve satiety by reducing cravings, thereby treating obesity. Black walnut husk extract is antifungal. An antifungal compound: Equal parts of tincture of golden seal, cinnamon, tea tree oil, and black walnut husk tincture.

Edible Plants of the Mountain West

ARROW-LEAFED BALSAMROOT

Asteraceae (*Balsamorhiza* spp.)
Identification: Found in clumps and colonies, these plants have arrow-shaped, basal leaves, 8"–12" in length. Leaves are hairy, rough to the touch. Flowers are yellow and long stalked. Up to 22 yellow rays encircle the yellow disc of florets.

Habitat: Grows on dry, stony slopes in the foothills and higher elevation of the Rockies from Colorado to British Columbia—widespread in the Bitterroots and other Idaho wilderness areas. Find balsamroot on the hike from Pebble Creek Campground in Yellowstone to the confluence of the Lamar River and Cache Creek (take along your fly rod).

Food uses: Young leaves and shoots are edible, as well as young flower stalks and young stems. They may be steamed or eaten raw. Peeled roots eaten, but taste bitter unless slow cooked to break down the indigestible polysaccharide (inulin). Roots may be cooked and dried, then reconstituted in simmering water before eating. Eat seeds out of hand or pounded into meal and used as flour. The roasted seeds can be ground into pinole. The Nez Percé Indians roasted and ground the seeds, which they then formed into little balls by adding grease. In a pinch (should you get lost in these vast mountainous expanses), here is a readily available survival food—but freeing the root, often deeply and intricately woven into the rock, is an exhausting task.

Medicinal uses: Native Americans used the wet leaves as a wound dressing and a poultice over burns. The sticky sap was used to seal wounds and considered antiseptic. Balsamroot, when peeled and chewed, although bitter, contains inulin that may stimulate the immune system, providing protection from acute sickness, such as colds and flu. The sap is considered antibacterial and antifungal. A decoction of the leaves, stems, and roots administered for stomachache, colds. Root traditionally used for treating gonorrhea and syphilis. In sweat lodges, balsamroot smoke and steam said to relieve headaches. Considered a warrior plant in smudging ceremonies and a disinfectant; the inhaled smoke was said to relieve body aches. Chewed root used as a poultice over sores, wounds, and burns. Whole plant decocted for stomach pain.

AVALANCHE LILY, YELLOW AVALANCHE LILY, GLACIER LILY

Liliaceae (*Erythronium grandiflorum* and other species)

Identification: Leaves lance and ellipse shaped, narrowing at base, with a deeply buried, edible corm. Single yellow flower (sometimes 2) on 7" or 8" stem (blooms in June and July).

Habitat: Found in alpine meadows and high slopes in western mountains. These species are similar to, and from the same genus as, the trout lily (dogtooth violet) of the eastern United States but are more sun tolerant.

Food uses: Reaching the corm is a difficult dig, requiring much effort. Native Americans wrapped the bulbs in cattails and reeds, then cooked them in an earth-filled pit over which a fire was burned; 10–12 hours in the pit would render the corms both edible and delicious.

> *Warning: The corm contains the polysaccharide inulin—cook to make digestible. Plant protected in most areas, so buy the roots online at herbs .com or Pacific Botanicals (pacificbotanicals.com).*

Medicinal uses: The inulin-rich bulb may be therapeutic to diabetics. (In Japan the inulin in burdock root is used to treat diabetics.)

BEARGRASS, TURKEY BEARD, ELK GRASS

Liliaceae (*Xerophyllum tenax*)

Identification: Grasslike member of the lily family that grows as a clump of wiry, elongated, sharply pointed, saw-toothed blades to 2' in height. As it matures, an unbranched central stalk emerges, producing a terminal raceme (pyramidal cluster) of white flowers. Often found in groups, with several plants emanating from a single elongated rhizome, the plant produces 1 cluster of flowers before dying back.

Habitat: Found on mountain slopes to the timber line, from Alaska south to northern California. I have seen ample amounts near the tree line on Mount Rainier, en route to the Burroughs at Sunrise, the northwest entrance to the park.

Food uses: Roots may be gathered and boiled or roasted until tender. Although not delicious, and for some not even good, it may be the psychological lift one needs in a survival situation.

Note: Fragile beargrass is a barometer of ecosystem quality, and it is vanishing from numerous habitats—use only as a survival food. Florists gather leaves as filler for bouquets.

Medicinal uses: Native Americans chewed the roots and applied them as a poultice over wounds. Claimed to be hemostatic (stops bleeding). Roots chopped fine and prepared in decoction to treat broken bones and sprains. Roots have saponins, surfactant wetting agents that are used as a lather over wounds. For further reference, see Daniel Moerman's *Native American Ethnobotany.*

MEADOW BISTORT, ALPINE BISTORT, LADY'S THUMB

Polygonaceae (*Polygonum bistortoides, P. viviparum, P. persicaria*)

Identification: Erect herb to 30", with lance-shaped basal leaves, flowers on erect stalk, producing brownish achenes (seeds). Flowers white in single dense cluster atop stalk, later forming a seed head.

Polygonum seed salad

Habitat: *P. bistortoides* and *P. vivparum* grow on wet, open slopes; abundant in the alpine meadows of Mount Rainier, the Cascades, from New Mexico to Alaska. South of Bozeman, Montana, on the Mirror Lake Trail, bistort spreads in abundance. Around 6 p.m. have your fly rod handy as the grayling feed on the surface for a furious hour of catch-and-release fishing. *P. persicaria* is found both east and west of the Mississippi in drier areas: vacant lots, meadows, and wet areas, including my garden.

Polygonum spp.

Notes: Easily identified and harvested in areas where harvesting is allowed.

Food uses: Young leaves and shoots edible raw or sautéed in butter; slightly sour taste—older leaves tough and stringy. Leaves in salads and cooked with meat. Starchy root is edible, boiled in soups and stews, or soaked in water, dried and pounded (ground) into flour for biscuits, rolls, bread. Cooked roots said to taste like almonds, chestnuts. Seeds are edible and pleasant tasting.

P. bistortoides

Medicinal uses: Vitamin C–rich plant used to treat or prevent scurvy. Alcohol tincture is astringent and used externally on cuts, abrasions, pimples, insect stings and bites, inflammation, and infections. Little used today as a medicinal. Traditional uses still employed by montane-dwelling Native Americans and Europeans.

BLUEBELLS, CHIMING BELLS

Boraginaceae (*Mertensia* spp.)

Identification: Numerous species bear numerous blue (sometimes pinkish-blue) bell-shaped flowers (1" in length), that droop and, in a generous wind, appear to be ringing. Petals are fused. Succulent lance-shaped leaves are alternate, climbing the sturdy stem, and as they approach the cluster of flowers, appear to be almost opposite. Plants spread in profuse colonies.

Habitat: Taller species prefer moist meadows and stream banks, shorelines, seeps. Smaller subalpine and alpine species tolerate drier conditions. Meadows of chiming bells dominate the wet areas of East Ten Sleep Creek in the Bighorns of Wyoming.

Food uses: Leaves have an unusual and palatable flavor raw, steamed, or sautéed. Eat in moderation, as plant concentrates minerals, both good and bad.

Medicinal uses: Tea of aerial parts infused and taken to increase lactation. Infusion of leaves also used to treat symptoms of smallpox and measles.

DEVIL'S CLUB

Araliaceae (*Oplopanax horridus*)

Identification: Shrubby perennial to 10', a twisted tangle of spiny thorns. Has a sweet odor and displays large maple-like leaves armed on the underside with thorns. White flowers grouped in a club-like terminal head.

Habitat: Western mountains to the West Coast, especially in wet areas: seeps, stream banks, moist, low-lying forests—prevalent in the Olympic Range and Cascades, from sea level to the tree line in Canada.

Food uses: Berries inedible, but spring buds eaten as a survival food (meaning in hard times, people eat dirt). Pick young shoots with soft spines; get there early, right after the snow clears. This armored plant walls off every environment it loves.

Medicinal uses: One of the most important medicinal plants of the West; roots, berries, and greenish bark are used. Berries rubbed in hair to kill lice and create a shine. Inner bark chewed raw as a purgative, or decocted and imbibed for the same reason. Infused inner bark taken to relieve bowel, stomach cramps; arthritis; and ulcers. For further reference see the author's *Medicinal Plants of North America*.

ELK THISTLE

Asteraceae (*Cirsium scariosum*)

Identification: Spiny leaves in whorls around stem. Stem single spike studded with spines and spiny leaves. Purple flowers are born on the apex of the stem, flowers to 1½" wide.

Habitat: This thistle is abundant in meadows, subalpine and alpine lowlands in the Mountain West, especially abundant around Yellowstone. Found in Wyoming, Montana, Idaho, Washington, Colorado.

Food uses: Roots of elk thistle (also called meadow thistle) may be eaten raw, roasted, fried, pit-baked. Native Americans pit-baked the root. Knife this plant where it stands, cut away spines and skin, and eat core.

Medicinal uses: Roots of this thistle and others used as a poultice over wounds, swellings. Root decoction used for many purposes to include treating back pain. Whole plant smudged for treating headaches.

FIREWEED

Onagraceae (*Epilobium angustifolium, E. latifolia*)

Identification: Tall stem with narrow lance-shaped leaves that alternate, rising to a spire of pink flowers. Found singly or in colonies in burned out areas, on disturbed ground, and along roadsides of the West. Erect stem bears a spired cluster of flowers with 4 petals. Leaf veins form loops that are distinctive, leaves paler underneath, darker on top. Seedpods borne on spire, mature and release airborne fluffy seeds. Blooms form April through August, dependent on altitude.

Habitat: Burnouts, roadsides, disturbed areas in profusion, more sparsely elsewhere. Tolerates damp and dry areas, lowlands and highlands, some shade, but prefers drier areas, full sun.

Food uses: Edible flower, raw or cooked. Vitamin-rich leaves and tender shoots of early growth are steamed, sautéed, or stir-fried. Add tender young leaves to salads. Shoots pushing up from the ground are tasty, tender, and worth discovering.

Medicinal uses: Intense infusion of whole plant used as a laxative. Leaf and flower tea considered antispasmodic. Root chewed and used as a poultice over wounds. Whole herb tea used to treat candidiasis.

GERANIUM
Geraniaceae (*Geranium viscosissimum* and other *Geranium* species)
Identification: Showy flowers with 5 petals from pale white to pink and purple. Plant grows to 3' but is usually smaller, in colonies, mixed with other wildflowers. Leaves are deeply cut, palmate, and plentiful. Plant blooms April–July, even into August at higher altitudes.

Habitat: Meadow varieties, alpine dwellers and subalpine relatives, near water sources in abundance at West Ten Sleep Campground in the Bighorns off Highway 16 and Hyalite Canyon around Mirror Lake. Found in wet areas, grasslands, and around ponds and seeps.

Food uses: Sauté, or eat the flowers raw on the hoof. I avoid leaves, as they are more astringent, but when astringency is desirable, use prudently. Although not a favorite, this flower is abundant and can make the difference in a survival scenario.

Medicinal uses: Root decoction said to stem diarrhea. Leaf infusion, cooled and used as a gargle. Decoctions of the aerial parts of the plant used by several Native American tribes as a "life medicine"—a panacea, if you will, to treat internal ailments. Dried leaves used as a snuff to stem nosebleeds.

HAREBELLS
Campanulaceae (*Campanula* spp.)
Identification: Delicate bell-shaped blue to lavender-blue flower (petals partially fused) on delicate stem, with delicate, simple, and extremely narrow leaves. Leaves are alternate. Plant grows 8"–12" tall when mature and blooms April–August, depending on latitude and altitude (and possibly attitude).

Habitat: Found in drier foothills and benches of western mountains. Quickly found on the American Serengeti, the broad overreaching meadows of the Lamar River valley in Yellowstone. (Forgot your fly rod? Too bad.)

Food uses: Boil or sauté roots—a fireside nibble. When hiking I eat a flower or 2 just to say I did it.

Medicinal uses: Infusion of eastern species used by Native Americans to treat whooping cough and tuberculosis.

LICORICE

Fabaceae (*Glycyrrhiza lepidota*)
Identification: 3'-tall (plus or minus) perennial, with pinnately divided compound leaves with 11–19 leaflets. Leaflets are lance-shaped to about 1½" in length. Flowers are yellowish to green-white, pealike to ½", bearing a burr-like fruit that is brown, covered with Velcro-like bristles, and is indicative of the plant.

Habitat: Found in moist, well-drained areas. A favorite foraging spot is near the riverside campground along the edges of the North Fork of the Shoshone, just above Buffalo Bill Reservoir in Wyoming, 10 miles west of Cody.

Food uses: Like Oriental licorice, the roots eaten raw or roasted in moderation, and then pounded and sucked or eaten—use to flavor deserts and confections. Glycyrrhizin in the root is sweeter than sugar and said to quench thirst. Like the Oriental variety, use this herb in moderation, as its chemistry is steroidal and may raise blood pressure.

Medicinal uses: Chewed leaves applied as poultice. Root used to settle stomach, a soothing demulcent for the digestive tract. Root also used to treat ulcers and arthritis. Like Oriental variety, used to regulate menses. Raw root juice gargled to reduce toothache. Mucilaginous root soothes throat and suppresses coughs. Steroidal-like compounds in root act similar to store-purchased licorice in Asian markets.

Caution: Prolonged or substantive use may raise blood pressure and have other undesirable steroidal effects.

MARSH MARIGOLD, ELKSLIP

Ranunculaceae (*Caltha leptosepala*)
Identification: Fleshy basal leaves, oblong and heart-shaped leaves. Flowers white or white and bluish tinged to 1½" in diameter, 5 oval, oblong petal-like sepals, no petals borne on a 5"–7"-tall, sturdy stem. Yellow reproductive parts: pistils, stamens.

Habitat: This plant is abundant in western high places, along the edges of streams and seeps and alpine pot holes, ponds, and lakes, often in 1" or 2" of water. Find it on the trail along East Hyalite Creek in Hyalite Canyon and in the wet subalpine edges of the Bighorns. Also available in the upper reaches of Cache Creek, Yellowstone, and wet remote areas of the Cascades.

Food uses: Boil leaves and roots in 2 changes of water, then sauté in oil, margarine, or butter. Many sources finish the greens in sour cream or whole cream sauce. **Note:** Triple cooking leaves and roots reduces the toxic glycosides in the plant.

Medicinal uses: Masticated plant (aerial parts) applied to wounds (poultice) to reduce inflammation.

MINER'S LETTUCE
Portulacaceae (*Claytonia perfoliata*)
Identification: Leaves form cup or saucer around stems; delicate, small, white flowers. Found in moist, shady places.

Habitat: Pacific coastal range, east to plains. Particularly abundant near seeps in slot canyons of Utah, and along river and stream banks in Montana; tolerates shade.

Food uses: Cook like dandelion greens, or eat leaves and stems raw. Best cut into salads and laced with balsamic vinegar. High in vitamin A. Goes well with curly dock as a steamed green.

Medicinal uses: Tasty survival food, high in nutrients, and used as an appetite stimulant.

MINTS OF THE WEST
Lamiaceae (*Mentha arvensis,* *Mentha* spp.)
Identification: Aromatic herbs; leaves serrated (toothed); flowers in heads, or flowers in stem axils as in *Mentha arvensis;* stems square; flowers in clusters.

Habitat: Seeps, streamside, along hiking trails where water runs off, creeks, springs.

Note: The pictured mint was found on the climber's route in the Grand Tetons—a wonderful variety—fragrant and tasty.

Food uses: Add to sauces, pizzas, all bean dishes, chicken soup. Chew as a breath

Mentha arvensis

cleanser or brain stimulator. Add to game marinades; try leaves or flowers in bread and pancake batters.

Medicinal uses: Energizing tea, improves circulation to brain, helps ease altitude sickness—although thyme tea is more effective. Tea also cooling, lowers fever.

OXEYE DAISY
Compositae (*Chrysanthemum leucanthemum*)

Identification: Large daisy flower with white petals (up to 3" wide) and yellow center. Basal leaves are spoon shaped with long stems (petioles); teeth on leaf margins are round toothed. Leaves on upper mature plant lack petioles. Plant grows to 2'–3' and blooms throughout the summer. Early spring basal cluster of leaves are choice edibles.

Habitat: Found along roadsides, highways and byways, waste ground, meadows and fields; prefers drier areas. This European import has become widespread and a nuisance in the West. Get on your knees and start eating.

Food uses: Young basal leaves (which grow in abundance) are delicious fresh-picked in salads or sautéed—closely approximating the flavor of romaine and Bibb lettuce. Eat in abundance, as the locals and ranchers want to get rid of the weed.

Medicinal uses: Eating leaves and leaf tea is diuretic and may act as an antihistamine, to help relieve allergies and consequential mucus production. Leaves applied to wounds have a hemostatic quality and stem bleeding.

PINEAPPLE WEED
Compositae (*Matricaria matricarioides*)

Identification: Unlike cultivated chamomile, the domestic herb, pineapple weed has flowers without small white rays (petals) and a large yellow center of reproductive parts. It is spreading, many branched, with severely cut leaves; rayless flowers are conspicuous and pineapple scented, unmistakable.

Habitat: Widespread, along roadsides and in gravel roadways, pathways, waste ground, low- and highly impacted soils, throughout the country east to west, especially in the Northwest and mountainous areas of Montana, Wyoming, Idaho, and Utah.

Food uses: Tea: Fresh flowers preferred over dried. Fresh pineapple weed is more powerful than chamomile. Leaves are edible but bitter. Native Americans pulverized the dried plant and mixed it with meat and berries as a preservative.

Medicinal uses: Pioneers drank the fresh flower tea as an antispasmodic carminative to aid digestion, prevent ulcers, and relieve arthritis pain. The tea, said to soothe the nerves, may relieve toothache pain. Native Americans used the herb in the same way, primarily for relieving stomach pain, and they considered it a female plant, to be applied wet on hot rocks in sweat lodge as a soothing aromatic—inviting in the good spirits. Infusion of herb used to relieve menstrual cramps and relieve cold symptoms. Chamomile is widely used topically to treat abrasions, inflammations, eczema, and acne with varied success. One study suggests azulene in chamomile may stimulate liver regeneration. British scientists purport chamomile stimulates infection-fighting macrophages and B-lymphocytes of the human immune system. Commercial preparations in lotions and ointments used as antiseptic treatment of sore gums, wounds, raw or sore nipples, and other inflammations.

Note: A pineapple weed bath (1 cup flowers in a pair of pantyhose) makes an emollient, moisturizing skin wash. Inhaling the steam may relieve upper respiratory infection (sinusitis). Place ¼ cup fresh flowers in an 8-quart pan (containing 1 quart water off boil, plus fresh flowers). Drape a towel over your head, lower head to water, and inhale for sinus congestion. Washing hair with the tea improves quality and sheen.

> *Caution: Like many herbs, there is a paradox here; although antiallergic for some, pineapple weed may be allergenic to others, anaphylactic to a few. If allergic to ragweed, best avoid using this plant.*

SEGO LILY

Liliaceae (*Calochortus nuttallii*)

Identification: Deep-set bulb bears 4"–12" stem with grasslike leaves; flowers to 3" in width, white to cream colored typically, with 3 petals as wide as they are broad. Fruit is a narrow capsule, with 3 compartments bearing seeds.

Habitat: Found in dry montane areas from lower elevations to the timberline. Pictured plant found at 8,000' at Devil's Canyon Ranch in the Bighorn. Dryness of the environment and depth of bulb make this a difficult recovery.

Food uses: Credited for saving the Mormon pioneers in the fall of 1848, this survival food provides an edible bulb and edible leaves. But grasslike leaves provide little sustenance. Bulbs are best—peel and eat raw, or better, wrap in 2 folds of foil and leave in the coals overnight. Come morning, squeeze soft flesh inside an omelet. Hard-fried boletes are excellent with this breakfast. Seeds are ground into powder and used like cattail pollen, inside baked goods. Bulbs can be dried and used throughout winter. Bulbs can be peeled and candied, cooked in jelly, maple syrup, hypertonic sugar water. . . . Bulbs also edible throughout year, but best harvested in bloom until you can identify the plant in every season.

Medicinal uses: I believe, but have no proof, that the raw bulbs would kick up immune system activity, thereby providing some protection from acute infections like colds and flu.

SHOOTING STAR
Primulaceae (*Dodecatheon* spp.)
Identification: Pink to deep-purple flower, yellow at base, nodding on a long stem, 1–5 flowers per stem. Flower is dart shaped (thus shooting star), petals bending backward, whole plant 4"–10" tall. Leaves are ovate and basal.

Habitat: *Dodecatheon alpinum* (see photo) found to 11,000'; alpine flower preferring moist area along streams, seeps, weeping meadows dripping or draining into mountain lakes and creeks. Found throughout the northern mountain ranges from Montana to Washington.

Food uses: Entire plant is edible. Use only in survival situation if lost and without food. Eat leaves raw, roast roots, and munch on flowers. Eating a single flower will not kill the plant but may not be enough to sustain you.

Medicinal uses: Leaf infusion used to treat cold sores.

SITKA VALERIAN
Valerianaceae (*Valeriana sitchensis*)
Identification: Plant to 24" or more, blooms April through July, has a terminal cluster of white to cream-colored odiferous flowers. (Not a particularly pleasant odor to many, but I love it—that stink means I'm back on Mount Rainier.) Petals are feathery. Leaves opposite, staggered up the stem, often with several basal leaves.

Habitat: Montane plant, typically found on north-facing slopes; plentiful in alpine meadows and along trails in the Olympics, Cascades, North Cascades, Mount Rainier, Mount Baker, especially along Heliotrope Trail toward the climber's route.

Note: Take the road to the Sunrise Lodge on the north side of Mount Rainier, and walk to the learning-center garden to see this plant and many other medicinal plants of the West and Northwest.

Food uses: Edible roots not worth the effort; if you have had valerian tea, you catch my drift. But root tea is a mild sedative (sleep aid). Seeds may be parched and eaten. Prolonged cooking of roots dilutes offensive odor and saps taste—a survival food.

Medicinal uses: Root of plant in decoction used as a sedative—stress reducing, tension relieving for insomniacs. *Valeriana sitchensis* roots decocted in water also used to treat pain, treat colds. Poultice of root used to treat cuts, wounds, bruises, and inflammation. Root decoction also used to treat diarrhea.

WESTERN SKUNK CABBAGE

Araceae (*Lysichitum americanus*)

Identification: Large, green to yellow-green, elephant ear–like leaves that are lustrous and waxy in appearance with a "skunky" odor when torn. Much larger leaves than eastern variety; a small child could use one for a sleeping bag. Flower is an archaic showy sheath surrounding a club-like flower spike. Western skunk cabbage has yellow flower and larger leaves; leaves often 3' in length on Vancouver Island.

Habitat: Found as undercover in wet woods, swamps, lowlands, wet coastal areas, along the West Coast Trail of Vancouver Island, or the San Juan de Fuca Trail out of Sooke on Vancouver Island in British Columbia.

Food uses: Native Americans ate western skunk cabbage leaves and roots after washing and steaming or pit cooking until a mush-like consistency. Root can be dried, roasted, and ground into flour. Leaves placed over cooking vegetables as a spice. Young leaves, thoroughly dried, then cooked in soups.

Note: Several western tribes ate roots after boiling 8 times. Drying the leaves or roots of western skunk cabbage eliminates some of the peppery, hot taste of the calcium oxalate crystals. Calcium oxalate crystals (raphides) are toxic and make these plants, when fresh, unsuitable foods. The waxy leaves used as plates to eat off of, also to line cooking pits and cedar boxes used in cooking. Leaves are typically used to wrap meat and vegetables for pit-style cooking. Also used to store foods and cover fresh berries. Apparently the oxalate does not taint the food when prepared with raw leaves as a lining or covering. Never eat these plants fresh and uncooked. Roots are numerous and tentacle-like.

Caution: Oxalate crystals present and will burn your digestive tract if eaten raw and fresh.

Medicinal uses: Western skunk cabbage *(L. americanus)* used in the same way as eastern variety. Flowers were steamed and placed against joints to treat arthritis. In sweat lodges, warm leaves used as sitting mats to treat arthritis. Poultice of smashed root used on boils and abscesses. Root burned and smoke inhaled for treating nightmares, disrupted sleep, and flu. Leaves used as poultice for burns. Makah tribe chewed raw root to cause abortion. Charcoal of burned plants used on wounds. Steamed roots used to treat arthritis. A liquid extract of skunk cabbage is still used to treat bronchitis and asthma. Plant considered antispasmodic, expectorant, sedative, and diaphoretic.

Caution: Use reserved for skilled practitioners only!

Note: Botanical Beach in Port Renfrew, Vancouver Island, Canada, has some of the largest-leaved skunk cabbages I have ever seen. The leaf veins are tough enough to make emergency cordage or sutures.

WESTERN SPRING BEAUTY
Portulacaceae (*Claytonia lanceolata*)

Identification: This relative of the eastern variety has broader lance-shaped leaves, flowers with 5 petals, petals white or pink (with pink to red veins) borne on sturdier stems, providing a more robust appearance than its eastern cousin. A basal pair with long petioles, and narrow basal leaves die young and leave behind the mature plants with 2 broader, opposite leaves, below a stalk bearing 1–5 flowers—blooms April–July depending on latitude and altitude.

Habitat: Take a hike in mid-July from Hyalite Reservoir to Mirror Lake in Montana (trailhead 19 miles south of Bozeman) and discover this plant along the edges of the glacial lake surrounded by cliffs inhabited by mountain goats. Tolerates shade and full sun and prefers moist meadows and wet seeps from snowmelt runoff. Found from Montana and Wyoming high country to California, Washington, and up to Alaska.

Food uses: Like the eastern variety, the corms are tasty, with a somewhat bitter aftertaste. Eat corms (roots) raw, steamed or roasted. Leaves are edible raw or cooked; welcome addition to a mountain meadow salad.

Medicinal uses: Nothing in the record. Relaxes my mind when sitting on a log and chewing a corm. (Where's my cave?)

Edible Plants of the Desert

AGAVE

Agavaceae (*Agave* spp. to include American century plant, *Agave americana*)

Identification: Grayish-green desert plant, with long swordlike succulent leaves, to 10' in height—leaves and shape of plant similar to yucca but larger.

Habitat: Extreme southwestern United States, California, Arizona, Nevada, New Mexico, Mexico, Central and South America. Found in arboretums nationwide.

Food uses: American century plant roots are pit-cooked, crushed in water, and fermented. Young leaves are roasted and eaten (or stored). Fruit heads, young buds, and flower stalks are roasted and eaten (I have also eaten the flowers). Mescal agave "leaves" are cut out from center of plant, then "water" from the plant weeps into the hole. A pulque farmer, using a hollow calabash with a cow horn snout fused to one end, sucks watery sap into gourd. The sap is fermented in a bucket for 6 or 7 days, then served. Agave water is harvested in this way and is used as potable drinking water. Every Hispanic worth his salt (and a squirt of lime) grows an agave on his ground. Demand for tequila has greatly inflated its value. Disease is also threatening the crop, and urban sprawl in Mexico leaves less land available for cultivation. Agave brewed into pulque, vino mescal, and tequila, all of which as home brews gave me diarrhea. The core of the tender inner leaves of the plant may be cooked and eaten.

Medicinal uses: Agave water (juice, sap) considered anti-inflammatory, diuretic. The root extraction is an insecticide. Also, the fresh juice may raise metabolism and increase perspiration. Pulque (agave beer), mescal (agave fire water), and tequila (agave elixir) take the pressure off living.

Notes: The sap is used for treating and sealing wounds. Hernan Cortez dropped his ax halfway through his thigh and surely would have died had not the Mesoamerican natives stopped the bleeding and sealed the wound with agave sap, honey, and charcoal. The leaf was cut open, and the sticky sap was applied to the wound.

BUFFALO GOURD
Cucurbitaceae (*Cucurbita foetidissima*)

Identification: Annual, perennial herb; hairs on stems often hardened by calcium deposits. Stems trailing or climbing, tendrils generally 1 per node, stems often branched. Leaves simple, alternate, palmately lobed, and veined, with 3"–7" petioles; flowers at nodes, white to off-white or cream colored, and corolla cup-shaped, generally 5-lobed. Fruit 3" in diameter, round gourd or melon-like. Many seeded.

Habitat: Dry plains, semiarid areas of Southwest: Oklahoma, Texas, New Mexico, Arizona, Nevada, California. Found growing along and up fences, or sprawling along the ground. Very large plants covering up to a hundred square feet and more.

Food uses: What I call a survival food, because of its bitter principle, it produces oily protein-rich seeds that are edible after preparation. Seeds are 43 percent oil and 35 percent protein, making them an excellent choice for cultivation. Seeds dried, then roasted before eating. Unlike the pulp of the gourd, the seeds do not contain bitter glycosides: cucurbitacins. Be certain to clean all bitter pulp from seeds before roasting. Cook the seeds in oil or on an oil-sprayed pan over an open fire or in the oven. After 15 minutes of cooking, the protease inhibitors in the seeds are deactivated, making the seeds more digestible. Roasted seed coats may be digestible or you may remove them. Like the pumpkin seed, seed coat can be eaten (insoluble fiber) or removed. Seeds, like mesquite pods and seeds, may be dried and ground into flour. Roots are starch rich and may be smashed and then leached of their starch in water. Fibrous cellulose in roots is bitter; remove cellulose from starchy water to improve taste. Root water is fermented into an alcoholic beverage. This plant has commercial potential in arid biomes where there is a need for protein, starch, and oil. Bitterness is a problem with this survival food—if too bitter, do not eat.

Warning: A potentially toxic plant related to the edible squashes.

Medicinal uses: Dried hollow gourd used as a rhythm instrument in religious rituals. Ritual use may precede 10,000 years. Dried roots used as an emetic. Decoction of root used as a therapy for venereal disease.

Note: Saponins in root make for suds when pounded and mixed with water.

MORMAN TEA, JOINT FIR AND EPHEDRA, MA HUANG
Ephedraceae (*Ephedra viridis, E. sinica*)

Identification: There are several joint fir species. *Ephedra viridis* looks like it has lost all its leaves. It is a yellow-green plant, many jointed and twiggy, 1'–4' tall, with small leaf scales, and double seeded cones in autumn.

Habitat: Various species are found on dry, rocky soil or sand in dry and desert areas of the United States: Utah, Arizona, western New Mexico, Colorado, Nevada, California, Oregon.

Food uses: Native Americans roasted the seeds and then infused them into tea. Roasted and ground seeds were mixed with corn or wheat flour to make hot mush.

Medicinal uses: *E. viridis,* Mormon tea, was used in infusion as a tonic, laxative, to treat anemia, to treat backache, to stem diarrhea, for colds, to treat ulcers, and as therapy for the kidneys and bladder. The decoction or infusion considered a cleansing tonic (blood purifier). Dried and powdered stems used externally to treat wounds and sores. Powder moistened and applied to burns. In women's health, tea used by First People to stimulate delayed menstrual flow (dysmenorrhea). Seeds roasted before brewing into tea.

> ***Warning: E. sinica,*** *as a cardiovascular stimulant and central nervous system stimulant, this ephedra may be dangerous for people with elevated blood pressure, heart disease, and/or tachycardia. It is federally regulated and is not to be used during pregnancy or by nursing mothers. The import and use of this drug is restricted in several countries. Deaths have been associated with the abuse of this drug (100 mg may be lethal).*

PRICKLY PEAR
Cactaceae (*Opuntia* spp.)
Identification: All species are low-growing perennials and have an oval pad with thorny leaves of various sizes. Flowers are yellowish. Fruits are dull red to purple.

Habitat: Various species found from coast to coast in dry, sometimes sandy areas, even along the East Coast and on dry islands of the Pacific Northwest. The Badlands of South Dakota have prickly pear, as does the Sonoran Desert from British Columbia to Central Mexico. Great foraging found along the back roads of Texas.

Food uses: Pads are edible, and most edible species have flat joints between pads. Flowers and flower

buds are roasted and eaten. The pads, which are often mistaken for leaves (actually, the spines are the leaves), are edible. Plump pads thrown on hot coals of fire and roasted. The fire burns off the spines and cooks the interior. Let them cool, then peel the skin and eat the inner core. I like to slice the inner "meat" and stir-fry, or chop the pad "meat" into huevos rancheros with yucca blossoms and salsa verde. I have eaten the flowers of several species, as have Native American foragers, but there is little about this practice in the literature. So do so at your own risk. The fruit when red and ripe is tasty, often made into jelly. I like to eat it out of hand right off plant (avoid the prickly hairs). The pads mixed with water, sugar, yeast, and fermented into an alcoholic drink. The young fruit boiled and eaten by Pima Indians. Numerous other cacti are edible and often used as survival food in the desert.

Medicinal uses: Flowers are astringent and poulticed over wounds. Flowers in tea for treating stomach complaints including diarrhea and irritable bowel syndrome. The stem ash applied to burns and cuts. Pima Indians believed the edible pads are good for gastrointestinal complaints. Pima also stripped spines, cooked, sliced, and placed a poultice of the plant on breasts as a lactagogue. Leaf pads also sliced in half and used as poultice for cleansing and sealing wounds, infections, bites, stings, and snake envenomation. Pads scorched of spines, then slit, and the moist side placed against the insult or wound. The inner flesh, a chemotactic attractant (surfactant), draws serum from the wound site, cleaning and sealing it. Southwestern holistic practitioners report success in treating scorpion and recluse spider bites.

SAGE

Asteraceae (*Artemisia tridentate*)
Identification: Gray, fragrant shrub to 7'. Leaves are wedged shaped, lobed (3 teeth), broad at tip, tapering to the base. Yellow and brownish flowers form spreading, long, narrow clusters, blooming July–October. Seed is hairy achene.

Habitat: Desert plant, found in dry areas of Wyoming, Washington, Montana, Texas, New Mexico, California, Idaho, Oregon, Colorado.

Food uses: Seeds, raw or dried, ground into flour and eaten as a survival food. Seeds added to liqueurs for fragrance and flavor. Use as a spice or flavoring in small amounts as a substitute for salvia sage, good with venison, turkey, and chicken. Often sage is the only source of firewood in the desert. Most varieties of sage seeds used as food by Native Americans.

Medicinal uses: Native American medicine warrior plant used for smudging and sweeping to rid the victim of bad airs and evil spirits. Leaves used as a tea to treat infections, or as a wash for sore eyes, and as a tea to ease childbirth. Leaves soaked in water and used as a poultice over wounds. Tea used to treat stomachache. Limbs used as switches in sweat baths. Infusion used to treat sore throats, coughs, colds, bronchitis. Decoction or infusion used as a wash for sores, cuts, and pimples. Aromatic decoction of steaming herb inhaled for respiratory ailments and headaches. Decoction said to be internally antidiarrheal and externally antirheumatic. This panacea drug also drunk to relieve constipation. For details, see the DVD *Native American Medicine* at herbvideos.com.

Note: Add this herb to your hot bath, hot tub, or sweat lodge for a fragrant, disinfecting, and relaxing cleanse.

YUCCA

Agavaceae (*Yucca filamentosa, Yucca* spp.)

Identification: Common lawn ornamental, with long swordlike leaves to 2'; tough, fibrous, white flowers on a tall flower stalk, central to the plant, a striking and distinctive attribute.

Habitat: Almost universal in distribution (helped by landscapers and gardeners), various species in mountains, deserts, temperate areas; loves sun, tolerates drought, but does well on drained soil. Found coast to coast, north and south.

Food uses: Yucca flowers are edible. The young seedpods may be stir-fried. The flowers picked and sautéed in olive oil. Roll them into an omelet. Attractive addition to a salad, or eat out of hand.

Medicinal uses: Used for liver and gallbladder cleansing.

Note: I use the water extraction of the root to make an organic, water-soluble insect-repelling spray for fruit and vegetables. I spray pears with yucca root water in the spring. The results are excellent. Take about a cubic inch of root and blend it in 2 cups water. Strain, filter into sprayer. Add another pint of water and spray directly on buds, flowers, and young pears, apples.

Marine Vegetables

Almost all marine seaweeds are safe to consume, and the 2 questionable varieties are easy to avoid: foul-tasting **Lyngbya,** a thin, hairlike species that clings to mangrove roots in warm subtropical and tropical waters; and **Desmarestia,** which is found in deep, open waters and contains sulfuric acid and imparts an unpleasant lemon-like taste. Therefore, avoid mangrove-clinging seaweeds and deep-open-water varieties.

Because of limited space, only a few popular edible seaweeds are covered—by no means the limit of your foraging choices.

BEACH PEA
Fabaceae (*Lathyrus japonicus* **var.** *maritimus***)**

Identification: Marine coastal dweller that dawdles along upper littoral area of the beach. Beach pea leaves are compound, even numbered, typically 6–12 leaflets; leaflets tipped with a curling tendril typical of pea family; opposite leaflets about 2½" long. Fruit is pea pod–like and hairy, about 2½" long.

> *Warning: Many members of the pea family are potentially toxic. Make positive identification, eat only small amounts of edible wild foods, and follow all foraging rules.*

Habitat: Coastal areas of East and West Coasts. Found in sandy upper areas of beach among driftwood and dunes.

Food uses: Cook peas with salmon. Stir-fry, boil, or steam new growth (stalks of spring). After peas flower, tender young pods may be cooked and eaten like snow peas. The Inuits dried peas and roasted them like coffee, then percolated.

Medicinal uses: Chinese use peas as tonic for the urinary organs and intestinal tract. Eskimo (Inuit) consider the peas poisonous. Coastal Iroquois treated rheumatism with cooked whole young plant.

BLADDERWRACK, FUCUS, SEA WRACK
Fucaceae (*Fucus gardneri, Fuscus vesiculosis***)**

Identification: Bladderwrack, or fucus, is a perennial seaweed that thrives in wave-sheltered to moderately exposed conditions. The plant reaches 16" in length, and consists of many branches with little inflated bulbs at their tips.

The gas-filled vesicles on each side of the midrib vein float the plant in an upright position from its holdfast anchorage, enabling the plant to absorb nutrition and sunlight. Although a brown algae, color ranges from green to brown.

Habitat: Bladderwrack, a cold-water seaweed found in both the sublittoral (exposed at low tide) and the littoral (not exposed) tidal zones. It ranges in the Atlantic from New Jersey to Maine and north, and in the Pacific Oceans from California to Alaska. Gather from clean water free of heavy metals and other pollution. Forage at low tide in wave-sheltered coves and rocky niches.

Food uses: A common food in Japan, it is used as an additive and flavoring in various food products in Europe. It is dried and made into a nutritious tea, added to soups, particularly Japanese- and Chinese-style noodle soups. It flavors stews, fortifying them with iodine. I like to put a dried piece in my mouth and suck on it until soft, and then chew and swallow. For landlocked Midwesterners, the seaweed is available at Asian markets.

Medicinal uses: Bladderwrack is a component of tablets or powders used as nutritional supplements. It contains concentrations of iodine and is used as a treatment for hypothyroidism (underactive thyroid gland) and obesity. (**Note:** Amounts of iodine vary, making this a dubious use.) Bladderwrack contains alginic acid that swells upon contact with water. When taken orally, it forms a seal at the top of the stomach and is sold over the counter as a heartburn treatment and bulking laxative. Natural health enthusiasts also use the plant to treat dysmenorrhea.

KELP

Laminariaceae (*Laminaria* spp.)

Identification: A brown seaweed that can grow to more than 100' in length. Large frond-like leaves; stem can be thick as a human's wrist; air-filled bulbs or bladders hold plant erect in water. Plant torn loose and washed ashore after storms.

Habitat: Found along the West Coast, from California to Alaska, in 10'–100' of water.

Food uses: Excellent food for fiber and contains most minerals humans need. Wash the plant in clean water. Soak in weak wine vinegar or lemon juice until pliable. Air-dry in sun. After drying, scrape off blue-green surface layer. Kelp's thick white core can be chopped, shredded, or ground—best cooked in soups and stews. Dry the shredded

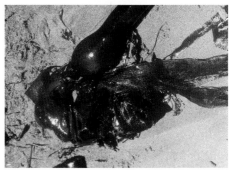

parts for later use. I have dried various seaweeds by spreading them on my car windshield in full sunlight.

Medicinal uses: Improves yolk color and calcium content when fed to chickens. Good source of iodine (important clotting agent). Kelp salt prevents muscle cramps.

Note: Gardeners are encouraged to spread seaweeds of all types on their organic gardens. Containing more than 90 minerals, marine algae are a wonderful addition to the garden.

NORI, LAVER, PORPHYRA

Bangiaceae (*Porphyra* spp.)

Identification: Rose pink to red brown with aging; flat, bladelike, irregular shape to 20"; satin sheen, thin, elastic.

Habitat: Mid–tidal zone.

Food uses: Forage in late spring. Sun-dry and store in airtight canning jars or plastic bags. When used fresh, season and tenderize in soy sauce. Sauté fresh and then add to pizza. Dry and flake into baked goods, or use in soups and stews.

Medicinal uses: May lower blood cholesterol levels (but as yet unproven) and is nearly 36 percent protein and high in iodine and vitamins A and C.

NARROW-LEAFED SEASIDE PLANTAIN, GOOSE TONGUE

Plantaginaceae (*Plantago maritima*)

Identification: Long, narrow, lance-shaped leaves growing from basal whorl; no basal sheath; leaves with thick longitudinal ribs. Plant's appearance is similar to narrow-leafed garden plantain (*P. lanceolata*).

Warning: Goose tongue can be confused with arrow grass. Arrow grass leaves are flat on one side and round on the other, with sheaves at the base of the leaves. Goose tongue leaves have prominent ribs and are more flattened. If you cut the goose tongue leaf in cross section, it would appear flat or slightly V-shaped. The characteristic plantain spike of goose tongue is distinctive. Remember Wild Plant Foraging Rule #1: Follow these 2 plants through an entire season before eating goose tongue.

Habitat: West coast of North America. Upper tidal zone or shoreline, often submerged at high tide.

Food uses: Succulently salty and mineral rich. Eat it fresh and raw. Also used as a stuffing for salmon. Mix it with finely sliced kelp, and sauté it with olive oil and water. Then stuff the mixture in the cavity of a cleaned and washed salmon and steam the fish in a reed basket or in a Chinese basket steamer over a pot of boiling water until done.

Medicinal uses: Fresh leaves and fresh juice considered anti-inflammatory and antimicrobial. Native American healer Patsy Clark chews the leaves and applies them over wounds. In Germany leaves are simmered in honey for 20 minutes to treat gastric ulcers.

SEA ASPARAGUS, AMERICAN GLASSWORT, SALTWORT
Chenopodiaceae (*Salicornia virginica, S. maritima*)

Identification: Fleshy mats. Individual plants grow from slender rhizomes; leaves are absent, reduced to tiny opposite scales; leafless stems are prostrate or erect, many jointed, with numerous flowering stems growing upright from the main stem; plant stems generally brown-purple. Eastern variety is emerald green in spring to red in late summer.

Habitat: Coastal areas, beaches, salt marshes in the upper tidal zone from Washington State north in the West and Nova Scotia south in the East.

Food uses: Wash and eat stems raw or cooked—salty. Eat like asparagus. Boil, sauté, or fry young stems. Older stems are not tender. Fresh plant can be purchased in seafood and grocery stores on the Washington and British Columbia coast. Native Americans dried and ground the plant and used it like flour in cakes and bread, typically sweetened with honey. Stems eaten as food by Salish, Heiltsuk, and Goshute First People.

Medicinal uses: External use (whole aerial parts of plants) by Heiltsuk peoples to treat edema, pain, arthritis, and rheumatism.

APPENDIX A: POISONOUS PLANTS

Here are a few poisonous plants for you to identify and remember. Several of these plants have long traditions in natural medicine but are best reserved for the skilled hands of a knowledgeable holistic health-care practitioner. See the FalconGuide *Medicinal Plants of North America* (by this author) for additional information. As mentioned earlier, many members of the buttercup family are considered toxic, and although a few varieties are eaten, I recommend you avoid them, as they are a novelty food and not particularly good tasting.

AMERICAN LIVERWORT
Ranunculaceae (*Hepatica americana*)
Liver-shaped leaves with hairy petioles; one of the first flowers of spring. Toxic alkaloid—avoid eating the plant.

ARROW ARUM
Araceae (*Peltandra virginica*)
Arrow-shaped leaf, pinnate veins; green primitive-looking flower; grows in water. All parts of the plant, including the flower and mature fruit, are toxic. I mistakenly ate a seed from arrow arum, and it almost ended my history. Compare the leaf veins of arrow arum with those of edible duck potato (arrowhead).

BANEBERRY, RED AND WHITE; BUGBANE
Ranunculaceae (*Actaea rubra, A. pachypoda*)
Actaea pachypoda has more rounded white flower clusters than *A. rubra*. Baneberry contains toxins that have an immediate sedative effect

White baneberry

Red baneberry

on human cardiac muscle. The berries are the most poisonous part of the plant. Ingestion of the berries can lead to cardiac arrest.

BITTERSWEET NIGHTSHADE
Solanaceae (*Solanum dulcamara*)
Climbing vine, found clinging to shrubs in wetlands, with purple rocket-shaped flowers, bearing a reddish-orange fruit with leaves lobed and alternate. Consumption rarely fatal.

BLUEFLAG, WILD IRIS
Iridaceae (*Iris versicolor*)
Wetland plant with swordlike leaves, blue flower; rhizome grows to about 3'. Stems typically have a gray-blue tint and are flat. Flower is orchidlike (irregular) blue to violet. Found in damp marshes, fens, bogs, along streams and the edges of lakes. It transplants to the garden and is resplendent. May induce vomiting.
Note: Prior to blooming, this wild iris can be confused with edible cattail shoots. Remember cattail stems do not have the gray to blue tint and are rounded instead of flat (see reference to *Herbal Odyssey* CD in Appendix C).

BUCKEYE, HORSE CHESTNUT
Hippocastanaceae (*Aesculus hippocastanum*)
Medium-size tree. Leaves compound with 5 leaflets, fine toothed. Fruit has husk with thick knobby spines, covering a shiny brown seed. Dried leaves and nut oil used as medicine. Nut is not edible. Active compounds are triterpene saponins, rutin, quercitrin, isoquercitrin. Traditional uses of dried leaves prepared in infusion to treat coughs, arthritis, rheumatism, varicose veins, leg pain such as from varicose veins or phlebitis. Infusions also used as a treatment for hemorrhoids and painful menstruation. Oil extract of seed used to treat venous insufficiency, swelling of the legs—a vascular tightening effect.

BUCKTHORN, CASCARA SAGRADA
Rhamnaceae (*Rhamnus* spp. and *R. purshiana*)
Small shrubs or trees, from 4' to 20' tall, many branched and densely foliated. When mature, bark is gray-brown with gray-white lenticels (spots). Leaves are thin, bladelike, and hairy on the ribs, fully margined, elliptical to ovate, and 2" in length. Greenish-white flowers are numerous and grow on axillary cymes. Flowers are very small, 5 petals. Ripe

fruit is red to black purple with 2 or 3 seeds. *R. purshiana* is taller, to 30', with leaves that have 20–24 veins. White flowers are in clusters. *Purshiana* grows in the foothills of British Columbia, Idaho, Washington, Montana, and Oregon. Another small shrub-like *Rhamnus* species grows throughout the dunelands of Lake Michigan. Berries eaten from a *Rhamnus* species I imbibed in the Midwest once ruined my anniversary dinner—severe diarrhea.

DATURA, JIMSONWEED
Solanaceae (*Datura stramonium, D. meteloides*)
Trumpetlike flower is distinctive. Seed capsule studded with spines. Flowers white to light violet. Leave are toothed, coarse textured. Found along roadsides and in bean and corn fields throughout the United States. *Datura meteloides,* more common in the Southwest and Four Corners, is a popular, showy garden flower throughout the Midwest. The plant is an unusual example of the Doctrine of Signatures (like cures like): With all its spines, the plant fairly screams at you, "Stay away!"

DUTCHMAN'S BREECHES
Papaveraceae (*Dicentra cucullaria*)
Deeply dissected leaves without a stalk, with white flower that looks like a man's breeches. Tuber is toxic. Rarely fatal, may cause convulsions.

FOXGLOVE, PURPLE FOXGLOVE

Scrophulariaceae (*Digitalis purpurea*)
Biennial 3'–5' with lance-shaped, fuzzy, and hairy leaves in basal rosette. Basal rosette of leaves looks somewhat like mullein leaves or comfrey leaves, rarely dock leaves—the leaves of digitalis are toxic. Thimble-shaped flowers on a spike, white to purple. They look like gloves, hence the name. Flowers bloom in summer of second year. Common mountain wildflower, found along roadsides in Northwest and eastern mountain states. This is a favorite ornamental in gardens from coast to coast.

HELLEBORE, FALSE

Liliaceae (*Veratrum viride*)
Large, ovate, stalkless leaves, clinging and spiraling up sturdy stem; flower yellow-green in branched clusters. In East grows in wet, swampy areas; in West found on open mountain slopes. Potentially fatal if eaten.

HEMLOCK, POISON

Umbelliferae (*Conium maculatum*)
Purple spotted, hollow stems; grows to 6' or 7' with white flowers in umbels that are either flat or umbrella shaped; leaves are divided parsley-like into small leaflets (like carrot leaves too). Plant has many characteristics of edible members of the parsley family. Ingestion of toxin, conine, can be and often is fatal.

HORSE NETTLE

Solanum (*Solanum carolinense*)
Leaves and stems with spines. Leaves coarse, irregular, large toothed; white flower with yellow reproductive parts. Alkaloid, solanum, causes vomiting, stomach and bowel pain.

JACK-IN-THE-PULPIT

Araceae (*Arisaema triphyllum*)
Flower is a spathe and spadix, and with little imagination you see preacher-in-a-pulpit. A dangerous and contraceptive herb if not prepared properly, and even at that, not palatable.

LARKSPUR, WESTERN

Ranunculaceae (*Delphinium glaucum*)
A poisonous plant defined by the flower color, evident spur, and shape of leaves (deeply cut). Various species found throughout United States. *D. glaucum* found in moist areas in the mountainous West.

LOBELIA, INDIAN TOBACCO, PUKEWEED

Campanulaceae (*Lobelia syphilitica* and other species)
Once used to treat syphilis, this member of the bluebell family has showy blue flowers about 1" in size found in leaf axils. Various species found across the continent, in woods, meadows, wetlands, mountains. Tubular and lipped flower is indicative. Toxic alkaloids.

MAYAPPLE

Berberidaceae (*Podophyllum peltatum*)
Woodland plant creates ground cover of large umbrella-like leaves. Parasol-like leaf deeply dissected, with a single white flower bearing an edible fruit in July. All other parts of the plant are toxic. Ingestion may lead to coma and death.

MILKWEED

Asclepiadaceae (*Asclepias syriaca* and other species)
Stomach-shaped seedpod, large ovate leaves that exude milk-like sap when damaged. Although flowers, young shoots, and seedpods eaten, with proper cooking (2 changes of water, then sauté), the toxic substance is a cardiac glycoside, and there are numerous other safe plant choices.

MOONSEED

Menispermaceae (*Menispermum canadense*)
Climbing vine with green stems, berries red when ripe and toxic, leaves round or heart shaped with a pointed tip; when not round, showing 3 shallow lobes (6"–10" wide). Unripe green fruit may be confused with wild grapes; ripe fruit is red—moon-shaped crescent on seed indicative—pluck seed from fruit to discover the crescent.

Cherokee used root decoction as a laxative, diuretic, and as treatment for venereal diseases and arthritis.

POISON IVY

Anacardiaceae (*Toxicodendron radicans*)
Climbing hairy vine, or shrub, leaflets in threes, with white or pale-yellow berries; contact causes dermatitis. Rub with jewelweed to reduce redness and itching. A thorough scrubbing with soap and water within an hour of contact prevents this discomfort.

POISON SUMAC
Anacardiaceae (*Rhus vernix*)
Shrub with compound leaves, 7–15 leaflets with white fruit (berries dangling
from delicate stems). Causes contact
dermatitis.

POKEWEED
Phytolaccaceae (*Phytolacca americana*)
Ovate leaves, pointed at tip; purple
stem when mature; elongated clusters
of purple berries. The plant grows in
gardens, wastelands, vacant lots, and
along the fringes of woods. Young
green leaves are edible after cooking in
change of water and then sautéing; pick
before stems turn purple for maximum
safety. Causes cramps and vomiting.

SKUNK CABBAGE
**Araceae (*Symplocarpus foetidus,
Lysichitum americanus*)**
Large, green, elephant ear–like leaves
that are lustrous and waxy in appearance
with a "skunky" odor when torn. Found as
undercover in wet woods, swamps, lowlands. Flower is an archaic showy sheath
surrounding club-like flower spike. Avoid
using the fresh parts of this plant as food
or medicine.

WATER HEMLOCK

Umbelliferae (*Cicuta maculata*)

Found near wetlands. Has sharply toothed leaves, white umbrella-shaped flower clusters, hollow stems, and in many ways similar to poison hemlock in appearance— and like a few of its edible family members. Distinctive is the leaf venation, which terminates within the marginal notches.
Note: Veins on water hemlock terminate at the notch instead of the tip. This is indicative.

WESTERN SKUNK CABBAGE

Araceae (*Lysichitum americanus*)

Lowland, wetland dweller has yellow flower; large, up to 3' leaves, waxy sheen; grows in colonies. Contains caustic oxalate crystals. Drying the leaves or roots of western or eastern skunk cabbage eliminates some of the peppery, hot taste of the calcium oxalate crystals. Calcium oxalate crystals (raphides) are toxic and makes these plants unsuitable as food.

YAUPON, YAUPON HOLLY

Aquifoliaceae (*Ilex vomitoria*)

Yaupon is an evergreen holly, shrub-like with glossy green leaves that have sharp points. Found in Texas and throughout the Southwest. Berries are toxic, not edible. Leaves and berries can be used to make dyes. The ripe red berries make a red dye in a mordant of alum. Use it on wool—place the wool item in the dye and let the color infuse in full sunlight. Achieve gray color by pounding leaves in water with iron and or copper.

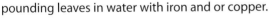

APPENDIX B: RECIPES

The secret to successful wild plant cooking is to start with traditional recipes that you enjoy. Try a dandelion leaf on a hamburger. Stuff miner's lettuce in an omelet. Add burdock root and Jerusalem artichokes to stew. Always add a sprig or 2 of wild mint to chicken and bean soups. Substitute what is available for what is in the following recipes—I dare you to do it. Become a wild foods wizard. You'll be rewarded with a long, happy, and healthy life.

Jungle Berry Toast

The best way to preserve and enjoy a fruit year-round is to make it into a jam or jelly.

Autumn olive makes a terrific jelly. Blackberry is second to none. Scoop pawpaw fruit from its skin, and spread on toast. Gather elderberries, cook them to a juice, and strain from their skin and seeds; add pectin, sugar, and follow the recipe. These recipes and more than a hundred more are found at herbvideos.com. Go to the index bar on the left of the page, and click "Recipes."

Toast wedges: blackberry, elderberry, pawpaw, and autumn olive. Drizzled with maple syrup.

Paleo Greens

SERVES 4

Combine 1 cup each of curly dock leaves, dandelion leaves, and stinging nettle leaves with 3 whole chopped wild leeks and 1 cup each of chopped lovage and French sorrel leaves (optional). Remember, dock, nettle, and watercress are available throughout the year. Miner's lettuce, nuts, and fruit are welcome additions to this dish. Experiment!

Combine chopped greens in a pan with ½ cup water and 3 tablespoons butter or olive oil and 1 teaspoon lite soy sauce; cover, steam for 2 to 3 minutes; toss twice. For added flavor, add chopped bacon or chopped smoked ham.

Crepe de Lasceau

SERVES 2

2 cups pancake batter
Cattail pollen
Morels
Violet petals
Maple syrup
Sour cream
Black walnuts, raspberries, blueberries, and/or mulberries

Crepe de Lasceau variation with blueberry, spearmint blossoms, hickory nuts, and autumn olive butter

Optional: Bacon, sausage, ham

Make a thin pancake batter and stir in cattail pollen (1 cup pollen to 4 cups batter). Sauté morels in butter. Cook a thin pancake (crepe) in a pan, add chopped morels and violet petals; roll crepe, wet with syrup, and plop—on goes the sour cream.

Sprinkle with black walnuts, raspberries, blueberries, and/or mulberries.

Piltdown Pizza
SERVES 4

Ingredients: Pizza dough, cattail pollen, wild greens (nettle, leeks, dandelion, plantain, garden sorrel, dock, burdock), oyster or other available mushrooms, oats, and flax seed. About ½ cup each of greens and 1½ cups sautéed mushrooms (whole or chopped). Olive oil. If you are foraging out West, flip on bistort, chiming bells, fireweed shoots, and geraniums.

Brown top under broiler for 1 minute.

Pizza dough: Mix 3 cups each of white and whole-wheat flour; add ¼ cup flax seeds, 1 tablespoon rolled oats, and 1 cup cattail male reproductive parts; add 2 tablespoons instant yeast to about 2 cups warm water. Add water and 1 tablespoon olive oil while mixing dough. Mix until you have a nice, semidry spongy ball. Cut ball into 3 pieces to make 3 pizzas; freeze what you don't use.

Sauce: For 1 pizza, 1 can of diced tomatoes. Pour into a saucepan and add basil, garlic, oregano, dill (to taste), and 1 teaspoon pickle juice. Simmer to thicken.

Cook dough in pizza pan at 500°F for about 3 minutes; pull, and add sauce and chopped wild foods (wild foods may be raw or cooked). Sprinkle on a combination of your favorite pizza cheeses, return to 500°F oven, and cook for 12 minutes or until cheese browns. Serve.

Neanderthal Buzz
This dish works well with oxeye daisy leaves and spring beauty corms.
SERVES 2

Ingredients: 3 cups watercress, 2 cups woodland or garden sorrel (substitute French sorrel), 1 cup chopped celery or young lovage leaves, 4 cups chicken broth (or mammoth broth if available), 6 chopped leeks (more if you date or are married to a Cro-Magnon), 1 cup sour cream, 1 tablespoon soy sauce, butter and olive oil, salt and pepper as needed.

Preparation: Sauté all vegetables in 1 tablespoon soy sauce, 3 tablespoons butter, and 3 tablespoons olive oil. Add greens and leeks to broth, simmer, cool, stir in sour cream—eat cold in cave, or reheat over the campfire and slurp. Powdered mushrooms change the taste of this soup but not the pleasure of eating it.

Hint: Top soup with several wild raspberries.

Frittata Archaeopteryx

SERVES 4–6

- 1 cup chopped nettle leaves
- ¾ cup chopped leeks with leaves
- ½ cup curly dock leaves
- ½ cup raw purslane
- ½ cup chopped watercress
- Olive oil
- 10 slices Jerusalem artichokes
- 7 thin or sliced spears wild asparagus
- 1 cup morels and/or sautéed wood ear mushrooms
- ½ cup mozzarella
- ½ cup Parmesan cheese
- 6 eggs whipped

Sauté chopped wild leaves in olive oil. Layer oiled iron skillet first with Jerusalem artichokes, then asparagus and mushrooms—add sautéed leaves, layer cheeses, pour over 6 whipped eggs, and cover with a heavy sprinkle of extra Parmesan on top. Preheat oven to 375°F, add pan full of ingredients; cook for about 12 minutes; brown cheesy top for 1 minute under broiler (watch closely). Substitute liberally: Shooting star petals, harebells, cinquefoil all work in this dish.

Serve with fresh or prepared salsa. (For more details see Tortilla Español recipe below.)

Velociraptor Pie

SERVES 4–6

- 4 sheets phyllo dough
- Cooking spray or butter
- 1 cup each: 2 strong-flavored cheeses: Asiago, Jarlsberg, Romano, Parmesan, etc. (2 cups total grated). I know, I know, it's a lot of cheese, but we prehominids don't even know what a heart attack is, and we work all the time.
- Generous additions of oregano, fennel leaves, basil
- 1 cup each: sautéed nettle leaves, dock leaves, watercress, leek leaves; seasonal mushroom—oyster and puffballs work great in combination. This is a mix-and-match creation—put in what is available, and see what happens.

In pie plate, layer 4 sheets of phyllo dough, one atop the other. Spray each sheet or brush with melted butter. Mix grated cheese and seasonings with wild vegetables and spoon all into the phyllo dough nest. Fold over tips of phyllo dough, to cover vegetables, and then spray or brush top with butter. Cook at 400°F until top is light brown.

Pteropod Pickles

Only a miserly Mousterian could come up with this: Buy a jar of "party stuffer olives." Pour pickling juice from jar into a saucepan, bring to a boil—meanwhile, stuff olives with wild leeks, wild asparagus bits, cooked chicken, mushroom pieces, and/or Jerusalem artichokes cuttings. Drop stuffed olives back into jar, pour boiling hot pickle juice over, and jar will self-seal—keep refrigerated. Leek-stuffed olives are terrific in a stone cup of Celtic gin and polar ice. Got pickling juice left over from a pickle jar? Then reheat to a boil and drop in all of the above, sans olives. Pickled wild foods enhance eggs, pizzas, sauces, sopa, and salsas—in any language the flavor is terrific.

Options: Burdock root, spring beauty corms, fireweed flowers, pokeweed greens, cattail shoots can all be stuffed and pickled.

Leek-stuffed olives

Lucy's Lasagna
Here is a modern twist on humankind's oldest recipe, created by our first mother: Lucy of the Rift Valley.
SERVES 4–6

Take your favorite lasagna recipe, but instead of spinach add sautéed leeks, dock, peppergrass seeds, watercress, and strips of burdock root—also oregano, basil, dill and fennel seeds, salt and pepper for seasoning. Stronger cheeses are best, and load up on sautéed mushrooms in season. Nuts and wild rice help this formula too.

Useful tip: First mix cheeses, i.e., ricotta, Parmesan, and cottage, together with spices and seasoning. Layer cheese blend with a blend of canned (or fresh) crushed plum tomatoes and a can of tomato sauce (fresh, organic, and local is best—ask any Neanderthal).

Homo Habilis Hontzontles
SERVES 1–2
3 dodo eggs, fresh,
    or 3 chicken eggs, fresh
Salsa—green and red and local
    (imported is fine)
4 stems lamb's quarter seeds per
    person, or flower spikes, about
    10" in length
Salt and pepper

Hontzontles with salsa, beans, mint flowers, Asiatic day flowers, evening primrose blossoms

Preparation: Whip eggs; dredge lamb's quarter seed heads through eggs until thoroughly soaked. Sift thin sheen of flour over egg batter; fry in oil (½ inch of canola or peanut oil) until brown. Pat dry on paper towel. Arrange on plate with salsa and black bean side; sprinkle with blackberries and sunflower petals and/or Jewelweed blossoms.

A side dish of wild rice and chopped leeks, stirred into salsa, supports enthusiasm for this recipe.

Mushroom Sauce Australopithecine

Crush air-dried puffballs into powder. This white powder, when reconstituted with water or broth, makes a strong-flavored sauce—unbeatable.
SERVES 4–6

> Any gravy mix will work—I prefer a turkey gravy mix. Use the hot water that you reconstituted the puffball in to rehydrate the gravy mix. Add oyster, chicken mushrooms, aborted entolomas, or honey mushrooms to the gravy.

> Dip toast points into the gravy, or use it as an effective styptic over a mastodon goring.

Magdalenian Mushrooms

SERVES 4

> Sauté 2 cups mushrooms de jour in butter and 3 tablespoons minced wild ginger root (Oriental ginger will work), cool, stir into sour cream, season with nutmeg (about ½ teaspoon). Use on soups, tacos, burritos, toast points, or as a chip dip—great on a serving of lamb or venison—rich too; *jawohl, das stimmt!*

Fungal Jim's Morel Mushroom Pâté (or Any Other Edible Mushroom)

SERVES 6

> 1½ ounces dried morel mushrooms (You may also use shiitake or other favorite
>   mushrooms.)
> 1 medium shallot
> 1 teaspoon garlic, minced finely
> 1 tablespoon olive oil
> 2 tablespoons vegetarian oyster sauce
> ½ cup soft yogurt
> ½ cup soft tofu

Soak dried mushrooms for about 1 hour or until rehydrated. Squeeze out excess water, then chop. Sauté mushrooms, shallots, garlic in a tablespoon of olive oil and oyster sauce.

Process (whip) ½ cup yogurt with ½ cup tofu.

Fold in sautéed mushrooms to make yogurt/tofu pâté. Goes great inside a Crepe de Lasceau (see above).

Leaky Fry Bread with Prickly Pear Sauce

This is a 2-to-1 mix—bread flour to skim milk. In the Paleolithic tradition, increase the fiber and protein of the fry bread by adding cattail pollen and flax seeds—a tablespoon of each, to a cup of flour.
SERVES 4

> Mix 1 cup whole-grain bread flour with slightly less than ½ cup skim milk. Knead mix over a board sprinkled with flour, fold 20 or so times (form a moist, firm dough ball). Pluck an egg-size ball from the dough, roll it out on a floured board with a rolling pin until it

forms a flat ⅛-inch-thick pancake of dough. Cut a slit or two into the fry bread dough. Place the pancake (fry bread dough) into 400°F oil (canola, peanut). Fry 5 or 6 seconds on each side (until the dough fills with air and browns slightly).

Prickly pear sauce made from the fruit. Press the juice from the fruits until you have a pint. Simmer until thickened slightly; add 1 tablespoon lime juice and a ½ cup sugar, stir. Pour hot prickly pear sauce over fry bread.

Tapas-Style Wild Plant Recipes

To be redundant, substitute what you have available in your area at your time of the year for the following ingredients. If it is a strong herb, use only a little, then balance the bitterness with something tart or sweet. These are taste-as-you-go recipes and withstand a great deal of sniffing, handling, and tasting.

Wild Leek and Poblano Guacamole
SERVES 4

1 large poblano pepper
7 wild leek bulbs
1 ripe peeled avocado, coarsely mashed
1 tablespoon chopped fresh cilantro
1 tablespoon mild salsa or 2 tablespoons chopped fresh tomato
Juice from ½ lime

Cut pepper in half lengthwise and broil until soft (turn frequently), then peel skin and chop.

Mash and chop wild leek bulbs, place in pan, cover with water (¼ inch), and simmer over medium heat until moisture is gone; remove immediately.

Add avocado, leeks, pepper, cilantro, and salsa (tomatoes) in mixing bowl, squeeze in lime juice, and combine. Salt to taste.

Wild Asparagus and Stinging Nettle Crostini
SERVES 3–4

1 loaf whole-wheat French bread
4 tablespoons olive oil
½ pound fresh wild asparagus
¼ pound chopped nettle tops
¼ pound finely chopped chickweed (or substitute chopped dandelion leaves)
¼ teaspoon salt and pepper, equal amounts
½ cup grated Asiago or Manchego cheese
2 fresh tomatoes, sliced
¼ cup Parmesan cheese

Slice bread loaf in half, brush cut half with olive oil, place under preheated broiler for 1 minute. Remove.

Cook coarsely chopped asparagus, nettle tops, and chickweed for 2 minutes in ½ inch boiling water. Add salt and pepper. Makes 2 cups.

Spread cooked wild vegetables on toasted side of bread. Top with grated Asiago cheese and broil for 1 minute or until cheese bubbles.

Top each crostini with half a slice of tomato, sprinkle with Parmesan, cut, and serve.

Wild Leek, Watercress, and Nettle Pie
SERVES 6

Cooking spray
2 cups whole wild leeks, chopped
Water
5 cups chopped watercress
2 cups chopped wild violet leaves
3 cups fresh arugula
5 cups chopped nettles
2 cups chopped chickweed
¾ cup fresh chopped fennel (bronze preferred)
½ cup ricotta cheese
½ cup grated elderberry wine cheese (available in gourmet supermarkets—made in Great Britain). If not available, use Fontinella or Asiago.
½ cup chopped fresh parsley
¼ cup chopped fresh dill or 2 tablespoons dried dill
½ teaspoon salt
½ teaspoon pepper
8 sheets phyllo dough, thawed
3 tablespoons chopped black walnuts garnish

Spray the bottom of a 6-quart pan (spaghetti boiling pan) with cooking spray, then sauté chopped leeks until slightly browned. Remove to colander and drain. Spray the pan again, then add 4 ounces water; fill the pan with the watercress, violet leaves, arugula, nettle, and chickweed, and simmer until wilted.

Use a colander to press moisture from all the vegetables including the leeks. Then in a large mixing bowl, combine the chopped (and uncooked) fennel with the cooked vegetables, the ricotta, and the grated cheeses. Mix in seasonings: parsley, dill, salt, pepper. Set aside.

Coat sheets of phyllo dough with cooking spray, press them into a 10-inch (oil-sprayed) pie dish. Arrange in a crisscross pattern. Gently press into the bottom and up the sides. Then spoon in vegetables and cheese mixture evenly. Fold ends of phyllo dough toward center of the pan, coat ends with cooking spray, and press to form shape.

Bake in a preheated oven at 375°F for 40 minutes (until golden brown). Sprinkle chopped nuts over and serve.

Watercress and Wild Leek Stir-Fry
Serves 2, or 6 small tapas dishes

  4 tablespoons stock (1 tablespoon seasoned rice wine vinegar, 3 tablespoons vegetarian stock)

  2 tablespoons peanut oil

  2 tablespoons chopped ginger

  ½ teaspoon brown sugar (optional)

  3 tablespoons low-salt soy sauce

  1 teaspoon dark sesame oil

  6 whole wild leeks (cut lengthwise, i.e., cut bulb in half)

  1 bunch watercress (cut away large stems and chop coarsely)

  2 teaspoons toasted sesame seeds

  3 tablespoons chopped cilantro

Combine stock, peanut oil, ginger, sugar, and soy sauce and swirl until hot in a wok or 12-inch frying pan. Add dark sesame oil and leeks, fry until tender (2 minutes). Add chopped watercress for 1 minute. Serve garnished with toasted sesame seeds and cilantro.

Options: Add or substitute chopped stinging nettle and chopped cattail shoots.

Wild Mushrooms with Wild Leeks and Stinging Nettles
Serves 2, or 6 tapas

  3 wild leeks, leaf and bulb

  1 tablespoon olive oil or canola spray

  6 spring morels, chopped

  3 cups chopped stinging nettle

  2 tablespoons water

  3 tablespoons walnuts, chopped and roasted

  3 tablespoons olive oil and 1 tablespoon aged red wine vinegar (combine as dressing)

  Salt and pepper

Sauté chopped leeks in olive oil for 1 minute, add chopped morels and stinging nettle and water; stir-fry for 2 minutes until steam wilts the stinging nettle. Serve hot or cold with toasted walnuts and olive oil and vinegar dressing. Salt and pepper to taste.

Options: Add watercress to this recipe. Also try with cattail shoots.

Tortilla Española with Morels, Jerusalem Artichokes, and Wild Asparagus
Serves 6, or 12 tapas

  3 Jerusalem artichokes sliced ¼ inch thick (enough to cover the bottom of a 10-inch iron skillet)

  12 asparagus shoots

  1 cup sliced roasted green, yellow, or red pepper (combine or your choice)

  ½ cup cleaned and coarsely chopped watercress

  1½ cups morel mushrooms, sliced (substitute available other edible mushrooms)

  6 whole eggs

1 teaspoon Lawry's salt or
   equivalent, or salt and pepper
3 tablespoons fresh chopped
   cilantro
¼ cup Parmesan cheese
Optional: ½ cup thinly sliced
   burdock root

Preheat oven to 350°F. Spray
bottom of iron skillet with nonstick
oil. Arrange slices of Jerusalem
artichokes across the bottom of the
pan, forming a base. Place asparagus
shoots above the artichokes like the

Tortilla española

spokes of a wheel. Spread roasted peppers over the first 2 layers, then a thin layer of
chopped watercress and mushrooms. Whip eggs, salt, pepper, and chopped cilantro
into a froth. Slowly pour the airy mix of eggs over the layers of vegetables in the skillet.
Sprinkle top liberally with Parmesan cheese. Cook for 15 minutes in the heated oven,
brown the top for about a minute under the broiler. Cut like a quiche and serve over a
corn tortilla with fresh salsa and refried beans.

Divorced* Eggs with Morels and Wild Leek (Ramps) Leaves

SERVES 1

2 tablespoons of finely chopped
   wild leek leaves
2 tablespoons minced watercress
1 morel, chopped
1 tablespoon butter
Salt and pepper
3 tablespoons green salsa
3 tablespoons red salsa
2 eggs
1 corn tortilla
1 teaspoon chopped cilantro
½ cup refried black beans

Red salsa recipe: Combine 1 cup
of chopped fresh tomatoes, 1 cup of
chopped onions, and half a jalapeño

Eggs up with wild currant and goose tongue (Plantago maritima)

pepper, minced. Add juice of half a lime, 3 minced wild leek bulbs, and 1 tablespoon
chopped cilantro. Salt and pepper to taste.

*Red salsa represents passion and anger, and green salsa is for naïveté or inexperience,
the colors of a failed marriage. Traditional Yucatecan breakfast.

Green salsa recipe: Boil 6 whole tomatillos until tender, about 5 minutes, in water at a boil. Cool tomatillos in ice water. Blend tomatillos with ½ cup chopped sweet onion (use countertop electric blender). Add ½ minced jalapeño pepper (optional) and juice of ¼ lime. Salt and pepper to taste.

Sauté chopped (minced) leek leaves, watercress, and morels in butter for 2 minutes. Salt and pepper to taste. Warm the 2 salsas in the microwave separately (do not mix). Divide chopped leeks and morels in half and add to salsas in equal amounts. Cook 2 eggs over easy. Pour green salsa over one egg and red salsa over other. Serve over an oil-fired corn tortilla, garnish with cilantro, and serve with a side of refried beans.

Vegetarian Beans with Wild Greens in Spring Stock
SERVES 4

1 cup chopped watercress
1 cup chopped wild leeks
1 cup chopped stinging nettle
1 cup chopped violet leaves
½ cup chopped dandelion leaves
1 cup chopped young (3 inches high) daylily shoots
2 quarts pure water
2 tablespoons vegetable bullion
1 clove garlic chopped
1 can black beans
1 can pinto beans
Sprig of epazote (optional)
Juice of 1 lime
1 teaspoon each dried oregano and basil
Soy or salt and pepper to taste

Coarsely chop greens. Add all ingredients to a saucepan with 2 quarts water. Bring to a boil; back off to a simmer for 15 minutes. Strain off the water and use for soup, stir-fry, anywhere vegetable-flavored water will enhance the cooking.

Wild Plants and Morel Vegetarian Lasagna
SERVES 4

½ cup cottage cheese
¾ cup Parmesan
½ cup ricotta
1 cup milk
½ teaspoon each dried parsley, thyme, chervil, thyme, oregano, basil
3 cloves garlic, chopped
1 (14–16-ounce) can tomato sauce
1 pound spinach pasta
8 coarsely chopped morel mushrooms
2 cups chopped stinging nettle
½ cup chopped wild leeks
1 cup finely chopped wild asparagus (domestic variety OK)

Combine cheeses and milk. In separate bowl combine dry seasonings and finely chopped garlic with the tomato sauce. Place a layer of **uncooked** dry lasagna in the bottom of an ovenproof dish. Ladle tomato sauce over lasagna. Sprinkle mushrooms, nettles, chopped leeks, and asparagus over sauce. Ladle a layer of cheese mixture over the vegetables. Add another layer of pasta, then repeat the sauce, vegetables, and cheese layers. Next, another layer of noodles, sauce, vegetables, cheeses.

Bake covered in a preheated 325°F oven for 45 minutes. Cool. Garnish with Parmesan cheese and chopped Italian parsley.

Wild Leeks with Anchovies Salad in Vinaigrette
SERVES 6–8
   ½ gallon water
   30 wild leeks
   3 hard-boiled eggs
   5 anchovies (soaked several times in freshwater to release salt)

To make vinaigrette:
   Juice of 1 lemon
   1 teaspoon chopped wild onion tops or, preferably, chives
   Salt and pepper
   4 tablespoons olive oil
   1 tablespoon finely chopped lovage (substitute 3 tablespoons chopped parsley)

Bring water to boil, add leeks, and simmer for 20 minutes. Combine vinaigrette ingredients. Cool leeks, dry, and refrigerate for half an hour. Peel and chop eggs coarse, and cut the anchovies into small bits. Spread cold leeks on a plate, drizzle with vinaigrette, and garnish with finely chopped anchovies and parsley.

Vegetarian Egg Roll with Wild Berries and Maple Syrup Salsa
SERVES 3–4
   ¼ cup Riesling wine
   3 tablespoons maple syrup
   ½ cup blueberries, raspberries, blackberries, autumn olives in combination or by themselves (substitute any other wild berry)
   ¼ cup dried elderberries
   2 tablespoons lemon juice
   1 tablespoons Dijon mustard
   1 tablespoons soy sauce
   1 tablespoon sesame seed oil
   12 prepared vegetarian egg rolls or pot stickers

Mix wine, syrup, berries, lemon juice, mustard, and soy. Bring to a boil, then simmer and reduce (mash berries into the salsa and cook until thick). Stir sesame seed oil into finished salsa. Steam pot stickers and/or egg rolls. Use maple salsa as dip, or drizzle over pot stickers and egg rolls.

Miso Burdock Soup with a Nasturtium Flower Garnish
SERVES 1

Vegetable bullion cube or vegetable stock
Miso soup base
1 burdock root
1 cup watercress

Prepare this soup according to your taste for miso. I like using the lighter mix, white miso: about a tablespoon to a cup of stock. Peel and slice thinly (⅛") the burdock root. Simmer the miso and burdock root for 10 minutes. Drop in a sprig or two of watercress for each cup. Simmer for 2 minutes. Serve with a dollop of sour cream, and garnish each bowl with 2 nasturtium blossoms and a feather of fennel leaf.

Marinated Lamb Shank with Jerusalem Artichoke Croquette
SERVES 2–4

Croquettes:

2 egg yolks
½ teaspoon chopped wild chives
1 cup Parmesan cheese
4 cups mashed Jerusalem artichokes
3 tablespoons flour
½ teaspoon pepper
1 egg, beaten
Bread crumbs or panko mix (add cattail pollen to fortify)
Peanut oil

Juniper-and-soy-marinated lamb shank with Jerusalem artichoke croquette

2 lamb shanks
¼ cup lite soy sauce
5 crushed juniper berries
¼ cup red wine (Cabernet or Burgundy)
½ teaspoon rosemary
1 tablespoon chopped ginger root (wild American or Oriental)

1 cup apple juice
½ cup beef broth

Croquette recipe: Beat 2 egg yolks, then stir in wild chives, Parmesan, mashed Jerusalem artichokes, flour, and pepper. Chill, then shape into squares or balls. Dip into a beaten egg and roll in bread crumbs or panko mix. Cook in a pan of peanut oil (about ½ inch oil) until brown on all sides.

Marinate lamb shanks in a large ziplock bag with soy sauce, crushed juniper berries, red wine, rosemary, and ginger root. (**Optional:** Add ¼ teaspoon herbes de Provence.) Marinate for at least 4 hours, up to 6, shaking bag every 2 hours. In a roasting pan, add apple juice and beef broth to the marinade and roast the shanks at 300°F until tender, about 3 hours—baste to keep moist. Serve with Jerusalem artichoike croquettes.

Option: Roast chunked root vegetables in the last hour with the lamb shanks: potato, sweet potato, rutabaga, parsnip, and onion.

Navajo Fry Bread
MAKES 4 FRY BREADS
    1 cup whole-grain flour
    ½ cup skim milk
    Canola or peanut oil

Mix 1 cup of whole-grain flour with slightly less than ½ cup skim milk.

Knead mix over a board sprinkled with flour. Fold 20 or so times (form a moist, firm dough ball).

Pluck an egg-size ball from the dough, roll it out on a floured board with a rolling pin until it forms a flat ⅛-inch pancake of dough.

Cut a slit or two into the fry bread dough.

Place the pancake (fry bread dough) into 400°F oil (canola, peanut).

Fry 5 or 6 seconds on each side (see the dough fill with air and brown slightly).

Jerusalem Artichoke Shoot Tempura

Break off early spring shoots of Jerusalem artichokes before the leaves open. Whip an egg (may leave out yolk), dip shoots in egg, drop in bag of rice or wheat flour, shake, coat, sauté, or deep-fry until golden.

Persimmon Pudding
SERVES 6
    1 cup persimmon pulp
    1 cup sugar
    3 eggs, beaten
    1 cup whole-wheat flour
    1 teaspoon baking powder
    ½ teaspoon cinnamon
    ½ teaspoon nutmeg
    ¼ pound butter
    1 cup milk
    ¼ cup black walnuts
    ¼ cup hickory nuts

Combine persimmon pulp with sugar, beat in eggs; mix flour and baking powder with cinnamon, nutmeg, butter, and milk. Mix all, including nuts, into persimmon base and then pour into a 9-inch, well-greased cake pan. Bake at 325°F for 35 minutes.

Italian Cream Cake with Hazelnuts, Black Walnuts, Blackberries, and Blueberries

Serves 8

- 5 egg whites
- 5 egg yolks
- 1 cup butter
- 1¾ cups sugar
- 2 cups white flour
- ½ teaspoon baking soda
- ½ teaspoon salt
- 1 cup black walnuts
- ½ cup chopped hazelnuts
- ¾ cup coconut
- 1 teaspoon vanilla
- 1⅛ cups sour milk (or buttermilk)

Garnish: blueberries, blackberries, and strawberries

Italian cream cake

To make the cake: Preheat oven to 350°F. Lightly grease and flour two 9-inch round cake pans. Separate the eggs. Beat the whites until soft peaks form, and set aside. Cream the egg yolks, butter, and sugar. Set aside. Take 2 bowls—one for the dry ingredients, and another for the milk and vanilla. In the bigger bowl combine the dry stuff—flour, baking soda, salt, nuts, and coconut. In the smaller bowl or tiny pitcher, add the vanilla to the sour milk or buttermilk (whatever you choose). Alternate adding the dry ingredients and the milk ingredients to the egg/butter/sugar you creamed together.

Now, fold in the egg whites. Pour the batter into prepared pans. Bake for about 20 to 25 minutes. Do the basic toothpick test to be sure they're done. When cool, slice each layer into two thinner layers.

The frosting: 4 cups powdered sugar (Sift it if lumpy!), 1 cup butter, 4 ounces cream cheese, 1 tablespoon rum (optional), ½ teaspoon vanilla, ½ cup orange marmalade (optional).

Frosting procedure: Beat together all the ingredients except marmalade. Set the orange marmalade in a cup or pitcher so you can pour it out slowly. Make certain your cake has cooled. For the middle layer, drizzle orange marmalade over the frosting. If you want to drizzle it on top, try warming it a bit first, and then it will be "drizzly"-looking instead of clumpy.

Compliments to Bill Fields.

Dried Salal Berry Cakes

Salal berries were an important traditional food of Native Americans of the Northwest. They gathered the berries and prepared them in cakes.

Serves 10

To make a fair facsimile of a dried cake, boil 8 cups berries until they are a soft mash, and then pour them into a greased cupcake pan. Fill each cupcake holder half full and bake at 200°F until the cakes dry (about 3½ hours). Reconstitute dried cakes with an overnight soak in the refrigerator.

Rabbit Stew with Juniper

SERVES 4

> 5 crushed juniper berries
> 3 cups chicken broth
> 3 tablespoons soy sauce
> 2 tablespoons dried and powdered
>   puffball mushroom
> ¼ cup Riesling wine
> 1 rabbit

Rabbit stew with juniper

Boil juniper berries, broth, soy sauce, puffball mushroom, and Riesling in a stockpot. Sauté rabbit, add it to the stock, and stew for 30 minutes. **Option:** Add wild veggies—like Jerusalem artichokes, wild leeks, and chopped burdock roots—in the last 10 minutes.

Hazelnut-Encrusted Chicken Breast with Raspberry Currant Sauce

SERVES 2

> 2 chicken breasts
> 1 cup ground hazelnuts
> 1 cup panko (Japanese bread crumbs)
> ¾ cup raspberries
> 3 tablespoons white wine vinegar
> 1 tablespoon sugar
> ½ cup safflower oil
> 3–6 teaspoons water

Hazelnut-encrusted chicken breast with raspberry currant sauce

Coat chicken with a mix of the ground hazelnuts and panko. Fry chicken.

Simmer raspberries, vinegar, sugar, oil, and water to reduce. Serve with the chicken, and enjoy.

Crab Cakes with Wild Leeks

SERVES 4–6

- 1 pound blue crab meat (or use Dungeness, rock, king, or other crab meat or a mixture)
- 8 saltine crackers
- 1 egg beaten
- 2 tablespoon mayonnaise
- 1 teaspoon mustard
- ¼ teaspoon Worcestershire
- ½ teaspoon Old Bay seasoning
- 10 wild leeks, finely chopped
- Salt to taste
- 1 tablespoon vegetable oil
- Juice of 1 lime or 6 slices of lime

Crab cake with chopped leeks and jewelweed shoots (Recipe at herbvideos.com.)

Put meat in a bowl and set aside. Crush crackers fine and mix with the next 7 ingredients. Gently fold in crab. Don't break up the crab into fine shreds. Shape 6 crab cakes, and refrigerate for at least 1 hour. Then heat about 2 tablespoons of vegetable oil in a non-stick frying pan. Sauté until golden brown on each side, about 3–5 minutes per side. Squeeze on lime juice or garnish with lime slices.

APPENDIX C: REFERENCES AND RESOURCES

Jim Meuninck has produced several 2-hour DVDs that identify and demonstrate the use of edible and medicinal wild plants. For free and useful information, visit his website, herbvideos.com.

DVDs

Cooking with Edible Flowers and Culinary Herbs. Jim Meuninck and Sinclair Philip (60 minutes/DVD). Herbvideos.com.

Diet for Natural Health. Jim Meuninck, Candace Corson, M.D., and Nancy Behnke Strasser, R. D. (60 minutes/DVD). One diet for disease prevention and weight control. Herbvideos.com.

Edible Wild Plants IV. Jim Meuninck and Dr. Jim Duke (2-hour DVD, 2013). More than 100 useful wild herbs documented, recipes demonstrated. Herbvideos.com.

Herbal Odyssey. Jim Meuninck (CD-ROM, 2005). Interactive media with World Wide Web links covering more than 500 herbs, edible plants, edible flowers, and medicinal plants. Herbvideos.com.

Herbvideos.com, Jim Meuninck's ethnobotany website. 3,500 pages of information and 1,500 photos, video.

Native American Medicine. Jim Meuninck, Patsy Clark, Estela Roman, and Theresa Barnes (2-hour DVD, 2005). Herbvideos.com.

Natural Health with Medicine Herbs and Healing Foods. Jim Meuninck, Ed Smith, and James Balch (60 minutes/DVD). Herbvideos.com.

Survival X. Jim Meuninck (2-hour DVD, 2011). Self-reliance and survival skills demonstrated. Herbvideos.com.

Books

American Indian Medicine. Virgil Vogel. Norman, OK: University of Oklahoma Press, 1970.

The Audubon Field Guide to North American Wild Flowers. New York: Alfred Knopf, Chanticleer Press Edition, 1992.

Edible and Medicinal Plants of the West. Gregory Tilford. Missoula, MT: Mountain Press Publishing, 1997.

Edible Native Plants of the Rocky Mountains. Harold D. Harrington. Albuquerque, NM: University of New Mexico Press, 1967.

Edible Wild Fruits and Nuts of Canada. Nancy Turner and Adam Szczawinski. Victoria, BC, Canada: National Museum of Natural Sciences, 1979.

Edible Wild Plants. Oliver Medsger. Collier Books, 1966.

Field Guide to Edible Wild Plants. Bradford Angier. Mechanicsburg, PA: Stackpole Books, 1974.

Field Guide to Medicinal Plants and Herbs of Eastern and Central North America, 2nd ed. Steven Foster and James Duke. New York: Houghton Mifflin, 2000.

Field Guide to North American Edible Wild Plants. Thomas Elias and Peter Dykeman. New York: Van Nostrand Reinhold, 1982.

Field Guide to North American Medicinal Plants. Jim Meuninck. Guilford, CT: FalconGuides, 2009.

Handbook of Edible Weeds. James A. Duke. Boca Raton, FL: CRC Press, 2001.

Handbook of Medicinal Herbs. James A. Duke. Boca Raton, FL: CRC Press, 2001.

Handbook of Northeastern Indian Medicinal Plants. James A. Duke. Lincoln, MA: Quarterman Publications, 1986.

Handbook of Nuts. James A. Duke. Boca Raton, FL: CRC Press, 2001.

An Instant Guide to Edible Plants. Pamela Forey and Cecilia Fitzsimons. Gramercy Books, 2001.

It's the Berries. Liz Anton and Beth Dooley. North Adams, MA: Storey Communications, 1988.

Medicinal and Other Uses of North American Plants. Charlotte Erichsen-Brown. Mineola, NY: Dover Publications, 1989.

Medicinal Plants of the Pacific West. Michael Moore. Santa Fe, NM: Red Crane Books, 1993.

Medicinal Wild Plants of the Prairie. Kelly Kindscher. Lawrence, KS: University Press of Kansas, 1992.

Michigan Trees. rev. and updated, Burton Barnes and Warren Wagner Jr. Ann Arbor, MI: University of Michigan Press, 2004.

Native American Ethnobotany. Daniel Moerman. Portland, OR: Timber Press, 1998.

Plants of Coastal British Columbia. Jim Pojar and Andy MacKinnon. Edmonton, Alberta, Canada: Lone Pine, 2004.

Sea Vegetables. Evelyn McConnaughey. Happy Camp, CA: Naturegraph Publishers, 1985.

Shellfish & Seaweed Harvests of Puget Sound. Daniel Cheney and Thomas Mumford Jr. Tacoma, WA: Puget Sound Books, 1986.

Sturtevant's Edible Plants of the World. U. P. Hedrick, ed. Mineola, NY: Dover Books, 1972.

Traditional Plant Foods of Canadian Indigenous People. Harriet Kuhnlein and Nancy Turner. New York: Macmillan, 1991.

Western Forests. Stephen Whitney. New York: Alfred A. Knopf, 1985.

Seed and Plant Resources, Catalogs, and Information

American Botanical Council (512-926-4900; herbalgram.org). Ask for their book catalog.

Horizon Herbs (541-846-6704; horizonherbs.com). Rare wild plants, both edible and medicinal.

J. L. Hudson, Seedsman Catalog (jlhudsonseeds.net). Rare and unusual seeds.

Richter's Herb Catalogue (905-640-6677; richters.com). A free catalog of edible and medicinal plant seeds and live plants.

Seeds of Change (888-762-4240; seedsofchange.com). Free catalog.

RECIPE INDEX

INDEX

ABOUT THE AUTHOR

Jim Meuninck, biologist, naturalist, writer, and lecturer, has authored four books and fourteen special-interest DVDs on edible wild plants, self-reliance, and alternative health. Now residing in Michigan, he has lived in four different countries, documenting indigenous culture on four continents. His favorite pastime is fly fishing, living with and admiring his wife, visiting his daughter and son-in-law, and discovering and preserving primitive technology. A few of Jim's DVDs include *Native American Medicine, Survival X,* and *Edible Wild Plants IV.* For more information on these programs and thousands of pages of free information, visit his informative website at Herbvideos.com. Jim's novel (five-star Amazon review), *God's Mistake . . . Never Give Up on a Bad Idea,* is available from Amazon and other retail outlets.